Radical
FAITH

Learning how to Trust
God Radically

Darryl E. Seay

Radical Faith – Learning how to Trust God Radically

Copyright © 2020 Darryl Seay
All rights reserved. No part of this book may be reproduced or transmitted in any form or by any means without written permission from the author.

Unless otherwise noted Scriptures taken from the Holy Bible, New International Version®, NIV®. Copyright © 1973, 1978, 1984, 2011 by Biblica, Inc.™ Used by permission of Zondervan. All rights reserved worldwide. www.zondervan.com The "NIV" and "New International Version" are trademarks registered in the United States Patent and Trademark Office by Biblica, Inc.™

Scripture taken from the NEW AMERICAN STANDARD BIBLE(R), ©1960,1962,1963,1968,1971,1972,1973,1975,1977,1995 by The Lockman Foundation. Used by permission.

ISBN: 978-1-7341169-6-0
Library of Congress Control Number: 2020902616
Printed in the United States of America

T.A.L.K. Publishing, LLC
talkconsulting.net

Dedication

This book is dedicated to three people who have taught me what radical faith is all about:

My mom: Delores M. Seay
You have lived in radical faith all my life.
Your life of faith has been a joy to watch.
I owe my faith to you.

My wife: Marla
Ours has truly been a journey of radical faith.
The way you trusted God in saying yes over 20 years ago still amazes me.
You are my Blessing and I love you eternally.

My daughter: Lydia Grace
Your life is a product of radical faith.
I pray that you will always trust God radically.

Preface

The Bible is a story of faith. It is filled with countless accounts of men and women who demonstrated faith in God. Both the Old and New Testaments provide many portraits of people believing God in extraordinary ways. Of all the portraits of faith found in the Bible, there is none greater than Abraham's. Abraham's faith was so radical that he has been called the father of faith. In fact, the three major faith traditions trace their origin through Abraham.

Faith is a difficult concept for many people to grasp. They see it as no more than belief. Yet faith is so much more than simple belief. Abraham's life demonstrates this clearly. He did much more than believe God at an elementary level. Abraham had such faith in God that he left all he knew to obey God's voice.

As we explore the life of Abraham, we will delve into his radical faith journey. We will trace his life from the time God called him to leave Haran to the day his journey was complete; when he offered Isaac as a sacrifice to God. There will be many principles that will help you on your faith journey. I am convinced that if you internalize and apply the principles, you will develop radical faith just like Abraham.

There are several elements that are contained within the book that will call for you to personally engage. These include challenge questions, time to pause and pray, and radical faith principles. Also, I have included personal stories of my own as well as the faith journey of others to help you along the way.

One literary device that may be helpful to know as you read is that I have intentionally used the name Abraham throughout the book. The goal is to prevent confusion while reading. Abram was the name Abraham was born with and was called by until God changed his name. Abraham is the name God gave him. May we all experience the blessing of receiving a new name as Abraham did.

It will be helpful to read Genesis chapters eleven through twenty-two along with the book to gain better insight into Abraham's faith journey. In reading each chapter of the book, you will notice I have included specific Bible passages. These are present to assist the reader in following Abraham's journey to radical faith.

Do not be afraid to challenge my conclusions or disagree with my assertions. I only ask that in doing so, you engage honestly with the text to gain insight into how I arrived at the place I did. I have never read a single book in which I agreed with everything the author said. I do not expect you to do so with me.

This is not an academic work. It is a spiritual work. It is not a theological work in the classic sense. It is a practical work concerning how we develop radical faith.

Now, let's start our journey together to radical faith!

This is not an academic work.
It is a spiritual work.
It is not a theological work in a traditional sense.
It is a practical work concerning how we develop radical faith.

─── *Let's Start Our Journey Together* ───

Radical Faith

Radical Faith: My Journey i

Our Journey Begins 3

How to Handle Faith Failures 17

Letting Lot Go 31

Preparing for the Blessing 45

God said it. That settles it. Now what? 61

The Price of Impatience 75

A New Name 87

Redeeming the Remmant 97

And Sarah Laughed 113

From Barren to Blessed 127

The Final Test 141

Radical Faith: My Journey

The year was 1998. I had been in ministry for six years. I had been saved since 1982. Almost immediately after accepting Jesus as my Lord and Savior, I knew I was called into ministry. After nearly ten years of running I finally said yes to the call in October of 1992. Fast forward to 1998. Now, I found myself amid a faith crisis. I was nearing the end of completing my Master of Divinity degree, was dealing with a major personal battle, and the Lord began speaking to me about radical faith.

The Lord often speaks to me is through scripture. He had me study the life of Abraham found in Genesis chapters 12-22. While studying these passages, God began speaking to me about what it meant to have radical faith. He deposited into my spirit a series of twelve sermons focusing on the life of Abraham and it was clear that Abraham's journey was my journey. The Lord was also clear that his journey was the one that all who truly desire to follow Him must take.

For the next twenty years I held these messages in my heart. I preached them once entirely in 2001 and have preached some of them throughout the last twenty years. What you are about to read is the story of a person of faith taking a journey over the past twenty years to radical faith. It is the story of a man who has learned to trust God in ways he never thought possible. It is the account of a person who has experienced faith failures, has had to let Lot go, has learned to trust God when the promise seemed impossible, and has often struggled to answer the question God said it, that settles it, now what? It is a personal story that will challenge you to examine your own faith.

To be transparent this story should have been told many years ago, but my own fear kept me from releasing it. I realize now that the delay has been part of my journey to radical faith. It has taken nearly twenty years for God to get me ready to trust Him that what He has done in my life will help others on their journey to radical faith. I pray it truly does help you as you read it.

As you read the chapters, please know that while you are reading about Abraham and his experiences, they represent my and your experiences. The journey to radical faith is always personal. God calls each of us to trust Him radically. He bids all of us to leave our place of comfort and familiarity and journey to a place where He is taking us. If you are ready, I invite you to join Abraham and me on the journey to radical faith.

Our Journey Begins

Faith: The Central Element of Christianity

Faith is the central element of Christianity. One cannot be saved; that is, one cannot be in a relationship with God through Christ Jesus without faith. For many of us, our faith is that which has kept us through the years. Yet I've discovered that for many people, their faith is ordinary. It is one of convenience and comfort. They think:

"As long as I can still live how I want to live, do what I want to do, go where I want to go, and say what I want to say, then I'll have faith."

However, in today's times, in these last days, ordinary, common, and traditional faith will not do. If we are to be the Christians God has called us to be and if we would see God use us to achieve His will in the earth, we need radical faith.

From Nothing to Something

The year was 2000. On the first Sunday in January Liberty and Truth Ministries was born. My wife Marla and I started the ministry with no committed members. She and I started based on the call God gave me. The call was clear—begin a ministry to meet the needs of the helpless, hopeless and hurting in Milwaukee. That first service we had about 35 people in attendance. No one was led to receive Christ or become a part of our new congregation. Yet I knew God called me to do this. We continued praying and on the first Sunday in February our first two disciples become a part of Liberty and Truth. To this day I am grateful for the two men who believed God and believed in the vision enough to become members. Both men have gone on to be with the Lord, but they are still a part of my story of radical faith.

"The LORD had said to Abram, "Leave your country, your people and your father's household and go to the land I will show you. I will make you into a great nation and I will bless you; I will make your name great, and you will be a blessing. I will bless those who bless you, and whoever curses you I will curse; and all peoples on earth will be blessed through you." So Abram left, as the LORD had told him; and Lot went with him. Abram was seventy-five years old when he set out from Haran. He took his wife Sarai, his nephew Lot, all the possessions they had accumulated and the people they had acquired in Haran, and they set out for the land of Canaan, and they arrived there. Abram traveled through the land as far as the site of the great tree of Moreh at Shechem. At that time the Canaanites were in the land. The LORD appeared to Abram and said, "To your offspring I will give this land." So he built an altar there to the LORD, who had appeared to him. From there he went on toward the hills east of Bethel and pitched his tent, with Bethel on the west and Ai on the east. There he built an altar to the LORD and called on the name of the LORD. Then Abram set out and continued toward the Negev (Genesis 12:1-9)."

"Now faith is the substance of things hoped for, the evidence of things not seen... and without faith it is impossible to please God, because anyone who comes to him must believe that he exists and that he rewards those who earnestly seek him (Hebrews 11:1 and 6)."

The Place of Comfort

Let us consider Abraham, the great patriarch of the faith. Abraham was the son of Terah. Terah was the clan leader of his group. Terah took his clan, his family, all his kindred, and all their possessions, to Haran. They left Ur of the Chaldeans and were now in Haran. They were on the way to Canaan, but they arrived at Haran and got stuck. They became comfortable in Haran. However, that wasn't their destination; it wasn't where they set out to go. They were going to Canaan, but when they arrived at Haran, they became comfortable. As you read the pages of this book ask yourself the question **"have I settled for what is comfortable?"** You were on your way to a place where God was taking you, when you arrived at a place of comfort, you settled down in that place, and now you've grown complacent. If that is the case God is saying, "I'm not satisfied with you being there." He is ready to take you to place of radical faith, and that's what happened with Abraham.

Terah lived 205 years and he died. When Terah died, Abraham had already lost his brother, so he was earmarked as the clan leader. It is important to understand something about the nomadic people of that day. These people were nomads. They traveled from place to place. So, their protection, their provision, and their prosperity depended on staying together. There was strength in numbers, in other words. Today that's how many of us are. The reason why we are so comfortable in our complacency is that we have found our strength in numbers. We may think, "Everybody's doing it therefore there is nothing wrong with having sex before marriage, with smoking marijuana, with same-sex relationships, after all it's how everyone else is living." Many believers have given in to the world's way of thinking and it is causing us to lose our spiritual power and influence. However, just because that's how everybody else acts, it doesn't mean that's how God would have us to act. There was strength in numbers which caused Terah and his family to become comfortable. You may be in a place of comfort, don't stay there! God wants to move you to a place of radical faith.

Disturbing the Comfortable

It sometimes takes major events in our lives to disturb our comfort. That is what happened with Abraham. When Terah died, God said to Abraham, "I want you to get up. Leave your country, your people, and your father's household, and go to a land I will show you." There are times when God allows some things and people to die before we're ready to move to radical faith. The reason some of us are in the same place we are today as we've been day after day, week after week, month after month, and year after year, is because we still have Terah in our lives. Terah represents your comfort zone. Terah is an easy place to be because it represents safety. Terah was just a man, and as a man, he was limited in his power. God is spirit and God has all power. The reason some of us are still stuck is that Terah is still in our lives and we think we're safe, secure, and free from problems.

But remember God didn't design you to live in Haran. He called you to Canaan. He called you to radical faith. God is saying, "*Get up and go!*" He is saying to you right now, "*It is time to get up and go. You've been in Haran long enough, you've gotten as comfortable as you can get, so it's time to go.*"

You might be asking the question, "Why would God, when Abraham had finally arrived tell him to leave?" He now had the position, the power, the prestige. Abraham had become the clan leader. He was the head honcho. The one that was large and in charge.

It was then that God said, "Go." I have heard it said that God disturbs the comfortable and comforts the disturbed. Therefore, if you have finally arrived where you wanted to be, if you finally have your life altogether, and you're beginning to see things happen God's word to you is, "Get up and go. I am disturbing your comfort." It does not matter how comfortable you are or that you are in a position of power. It really doesn't matter, because God is calling you to radical faith. It is important to know that you can't get what God has for you unless you go. You will hear this repeatedly, because we often fail to experience the freedom and fullness God has for us due to being stuck in our comfort zone. God disturbed Abraham's comfort by saying, "Go." Abraham had the position, the power, and the prestige. His protection, provision, and prosperity were even there. Despite all that, God said, "Go."

Spiritual principle: *When we reach the pinnacle of our position in a particular place, God always calls us higher.*

Let me say that in a different way. When you've gone as high as you can and as far as you can that's not where God wants you to stay and He will say, "Get up and go higher." As you read this chapter God may be telling you to go higher. I know it's comfortable but go higher. People are looking to you for answers but go higher. Your family finally seems to have it all together but go higher. Though your life seems to be exactly as you want it to be, you have not reached your destiny. God says go higher!

Blind Obedience: the First Step of Faith

After God told Abraham to leave everything, He said, "Go to a place where I will show you." God is an awesome God, but He also is presumptuous. He made a big assumption, because He didn't even tell Abraham where to go. Perhaps that is what you are experiencing in your life right now; God has told you to go to a place and He hasn't said where to go, He just said, "Go." Maybe the reason you haven't started the journey yet is that you don't know where He told you to go. The first step of faith is blind obedience. We must obey God even when we do not see the outcome of our obedience. The reason why some people never move to radical faith is that they will not obey God blindly.

The attitude of some is "If I can't see it, smell it, hear it, taste it, or feel it, I won't do it."

I call these five sense saints! But I want to let you know, radical faith is a faith of blind obedience. Abraham had no idea where God was telling him to go, but he had a promise. Today God is taking you somewhere and you have no idea where He's taking you, but you have a promise.

Listen to the promise God gave Abraham, "I will make you into a great nation. And I will bless you. I will make your name great, and you will be a blessing. I will bless those who bless you and whoever curses you, I will curse. And all the people on earth will be blessed through you." This is an awesome promise! Amen!

He has made us some promises also: He has promised "you are more than a conqueror (Romans 8:37)." He has promised "you are a royal priesthood, a holy nation, a people belonging to God (1 Peter 2:9)." He has promised "I will never leave or forsake you (Hebrews 13:5)." God has given us so many precious promises. He said, "all the promises of God are yes and amen (2 Corinthians 1:20)." Even though right now you can't see where God is taking you and you don't know exactly what direction He wants you to go in, I promise you, if you go, based on your faith He will get you to your destination. Trust in His precious promises and begin your journey toward radical faith.

Parting with Inherited Traditions

There are those who simply cannot imagine believing God in a radical way. There are several reasons for this, but the primary reason is a refusal to part with inherited traditions. Could you possibly be stuck in your traditions? The journey towards radical faith requires us to part with our inherited traditions. You have to part with what you've inherited if it does not allow you to trust God in a radical way.

If mamma's faith does not get you to radical faith, let it go.

If daddy's faith does not get you where you're trying to, go part with it.

Radical faith is something that you must get for yourself.

Abraham heard from God previously. He was living in Haran, minding his own business. Out of nowhere, here comes God and says to him, "Abraham I want you to get up and leave your country. Leave your people and leave your father's household. Leave everything and go to a place I will show you."

What happened next? Abraham said, "Hold on a minute God. We need to have a dialogue here." Or perhaps He said "Wait a minute, God, I don't know what You're talking about. Where do You want me to go?" We know that is not what Abraham said. God said, "Get up and go," and Abraham went. God said, "I want to take you somewhere," and Abraham went. He didn't dialogue, discuss, or debate. He just went!

The reason so many people are stuck is that when God gives a directive, we end up spending the next thirty years debating with God. Some have had a calling on their life for so long now that they have almost forgotten about it. Some knew ten years ago God was calling them to go to a new place and they are still in debate with God. For others, they God say *last year*, "I'm leading you to a higher place," yet you are still in the same place because you are debating instead of moving.

Abraham left! He did not allow his inherited traditions to keep him from responding to the voice of God. *Radical faith calls us to act when we hear the voice of God even when it does not make sense.* God's challenge to you as you read this book is to decide to part with your inherited traditions and act in radical faith even if it does not make sense. Will you accept the challenge?

> I remember when I came face to face went one of my inherited traditions. It was a Sunday evening when our congregation in Nashville gathered for a time of worship. I had been taught that women could not serve in ministry over men. I sat in the congregation as a fellow seminary student, who was on staff at our congregation stood to preach. I was not very open to what she would say, because I didn't really believe she should be preaching. As she ministered with word of God, I found myself in conflict with my tradition. I will never forget when the Lord gently said to me, "What are you going to do with your tradition now that you have seen me use this vessel to minister my word?" That evening I take another step toward radical faith!

Proving Our Personal Faithfulness

In addition to parting with inherited traditions, to develop radical faith we must prove our personal faithfulness. This means listening to the voice of God and acting on what He says. God will not force you to leave your comfort zone. You might decide that you're not willing to go. I remember very clearly having to prove my personal faithfulness.

> In 1999 I moved to Milwaukee, Wisconsin from Nashville, Tennessee because I was acting in radical faith. I had one job interview. I started off interviewing for an entry-level position and was hired to direct an entire program. When I was preparing to move, the Lord put it on my heart to birth a ministry. Once arriving in Milwaukee, I worked on the north side of the city and lived on the south side. As I drove to and from work daily, I saw all the churches along Fond du Lac

Avenue. I began questioning God; "Lord why did you call me to start a church in Milwaukee? There are already so many churches here, why do we need another one? After several months of questioning God, He finally one day said to me, "you said church, I said ministry. I've called you to meet the needs of those who are helpless, hopeless, and hurting. We birthed Liberty and Truth Ministries in January 2000. God has blessed the ministry that He birthed in me and in 2004 after just four years we purchased our first building. He has continued to add souls to the ministry and to change lives through the ministry simply because I believed Him at His word. God said it, that settles it, that's why I believe it!

This experience taught me the importance of personal faithfulness. I had to obey God and do what He called me to do, even if I didn't fully understand why He called me to do it. Personal faithfulness is obeying God even if you do not fully understand why He is calling you to do it.

I imagine when Abraham received the command and started packing, his family, friends, and neighbors thought he had lost his mind. Just imagine a cousin coming over, placing a loving hand on his should and saying, "Wait a minute, Abraham. Have you lost your mind? What do you mean, you're leaving? What? Don't you know that the Canaanites are going to attack you? They will destroy you. Don't you know there are ravenous wolves out there, Abraham? Don't you know that the enemy is going to come against you, Abraham? How are you going to leave? And think about Sarai! She's a woman. Who's going to protect her?" Despite all of that, Abraham left.

Even as you read this, God is calling you to a place of radical faith. He's calling you to move out into a place where you've never been. The Lord is calling you to prove your personal faithfulness. There may be people saying, "Hold on a minute. What do you mean you're quitting your job and devoting full time to the ministry? "What do you mean you are moving to South America to serve as a missionary?" What do you mean, you are giving your car away, because the Lord told you to do it? That's what radical faith is. It is proving your personal faithfulness even when no one else understands! Many people have this faith thing all wrong. Perhaps you remember the bumper sticker from a few years ago, that said, "God said it, I believe it, that settles it." The creator missed it a little. Really it should say "God said it, that settles it, therefore I believe it." The reality is when God says something, that settles it, whether we believe it or not. Abraham left. He got up. He started packing up. He started moving up and he went up to where God said go. He proved his personal faithfulness.

The Importance of Persistence

Abraham traveled to the land of Canaan. In fact, verse 5 tells us that is where he set out to go. "He set out for the land of Canaan and they arrived there." What is interesting about this is that in chapter 11 verse 31 we learn that when Terah (Abraham's father) left Ur of the Chaldeans, he was on his way to Canaan, but when they got to Haran, he became comfortable and stopped. What this says is that Abraham could have been in the promised land years earlier had Terah not become comfortable.

Spiritual principle: Our family can keep us from the place of radical faith because of their personal comfort.

God may have been trying to take you to a place of radical faith several years ago, but your family was comfortable in a certain place and because you wanted to honor your family, you stayed there. But now that God has set you free and called you to radical faith, go where He was taking you in the first place. This will take persistence and unyielding determination. Abraham set out and arrived in Canaan, the destination from the beginning. He then began traveling through the land looking for a good place to settle down. I encourage you to spiritually travel through the land and find a good place to settle down in your promised land. Perhaps you are wondering what this looks like. Settling down means learning to rest spiritually in the promises God has given you. It is trusting that the one who made the promise is faithful. It means feeling safe and secure in the place to which God has called you. In this place of settling down, there is peace and assurance of God's presence.

Radical faith calls us to persist until it happens. When you're moving toward radical faith it is necessary to develop a don't quit attitude. Radical faith causes us to say "I'm willing to trust God beyond reason. Even if the whole world turns their back on me, I'm still going to follow God." Radical faith says, "If I have to give up everything I have I'll follow God anywhere." That's the type of faith God to which God calls us.

The Promise of God

Spiritual Principle: *When God calls us to radical faith, He doesn't call us there empty-handed.*

God said to Abraham, "I will make you into a great nation and I will bless you; I will make your name great, and you will be a blessing. I will bless those who bless you, and whoever curses you I will curse; and all peoples on earth will be blessed through you (Genesis 12:2)." Then, just in case Abraham didn't understand that promise the scripture continues, "The LORD appeared to Abram and said, "To your offspring (Genesis 12:7)." Wait a minute, Abraham and Sarah had no children. Sarah was barren. They were childless. God said, "In your childlessness, because you have trusted me, I will give this land to your offspring." He made a promise to Abraham. When you trust God radically, He gives you promises. He says, "I'll increase your number. I'll increase your going in and going out. I'll make you the head and not the tail. You'll be the first and not the last. All your needs will be met. I'll give you the very desires of your heart. You shall prosper and be blessed if you shall trust Me."

It is important to notice that Abraham had not received the promise yet. He heard it. He knew what God said He would do. Yet on the Word of God Abraham acted, "So he built an altar there to the LORD, who had appeared to him (Genesis 12:7)." Radical faith calls us to worship God prior to the fulfillment of the promise. We cannot wait until God has done what He promised to start serving (*the word worship means to serve. See Romans 12:1*) Him. We serve Him until the promise is fully realized. We read "From there he went on toward the hills east of Bethel and pitched his tent, with Bethel on the west and Ai on the east. There he built an altar to the LORD and called on the name of the LORD (Genesis 12:8)." Abraham had heard from God. He knew that God was taking him to a place of radical faith. He knew that God had made him a promise that He was going to bless him even in his barrenness. He had not received the promise at this point. Yet, he worshipped God.

It gives God pleasure to bless you even in your barrenness. Currently, it may seem like everything in your life has dried up; like nothing is going right; and there's no life in you at all. Move toward radical faith because God has promised He will bless you in your barrenness with abundance. Worship God while you wait for the promise to come to pass like Abraham. Abraham believed God, built an altar, bowed down before God and began to worship. Imagine Abraham's thoughts "I haven't seen the promise fulfilled yet. I don't even know if He's really going to do it. But God said it, so I'm going to build an altar and bow down on my face before the Lord Most High. I'm going to call on His Name because I believe that if He said He will do it; He will bring it to completion."

Radical faith begins when we learn to worship and serve God even when we have not received what He has promised us yet.

Challenge questions:
Will you accept the challenge to move toward radical faith? Will you worship God although you haven't received the promise yet?

How to Handle Faith Failures

Radical Faith is Trusting God Completely

We are in the midst of a journey. The journey we're taking is to a known destination. God called each of us as individuals to journey toward radical faith. Radical faith allows and moves us to trust God blindly, to trust God beyond our ability to see, understand, and comprehend.

Whenever one takes a journey there will inevitably be unexpected detours. I call these detours faith failures. A faith failure is taking matters into one's own hands and momentarily getting off course spiritually. On the journey to radical faith it is important to know that there will be some detours. They are not designed to destroy your faith but to develop it. It is necessary to learn how to handle faith failures, so our faith is developed not destroyed.

I would like to say I've never had a faith failure or even that I have only had one faith failure. Yet there have been many faith failures during my journey to radical faith. One occurred in 2002 after preaching the Radical Faith sermon series. I sent them to be transcribed so that I could write the book you are now reading. When I received the transcription of the tapes back and saw the cost to convert them to a book, I became fearful. I thought I could not afford it. I tucked the information away thinking one day I will be able to afford to publish this book. God was clear with me that I was to publish the book because it would be a blessing to many. My fear caused me to doubt God. My faith failed! I pray you will learn from my experience and act in faith when God tells you to do something.

"Now there was a famine in the land, and Abram went down to Egypt to live there for a while because the famine was severe. As he was about to enter Egypt, he said to his wife Sarai, "I know what a beautiful woman you are. When the Egyptians see you, they will say, 'This is his wife.' Then they will kill me but will let you live. Say you are my sister, so that I will be treated well for your sake and my life will be spared because of you." When Abram came to Egypt, the Egyptians saw that she was a very beautiful woman. And when Pharaoh's officials saw her, they praised her to Pharaoh, and she was taken into his palace. He treated Abram well for her sake, and Abram acquired sheep and cattle, male and female donkeys, menservants and maidservants, and camels. But the LORD inflicted serious diseases on Pharaoh and his household because of Abram's wife Sarai. So Pharaoh summoned Abram. "What have you done to me?" he said. "Why didn't you tell me she was your wife? Why did you say, 'She is my sister,' so that I took her to be my wife? Now then, here is your wife. Take her and go!" Then Pharaoh gave orders about Abram to his men, and they sent him on his way, with his wife and everything he had." Genesis 12:10-20

Defining Faith Failures

Radical faith is learning to depend on God completely. In order to develop radical faith, we must daily surrender our will to God. As we journey to radical faith, there will be times when our faith fails. Let's define a faith failure more completely. *A faith failure is knowing what it is that God has called us to do, be, or say, but failing to do, be, or say it. Simply put, a faith failure is failing to believe God at God's Word.* Maybe you're not experiencing a faith failure today, but if you continue the journey to radical faith there will come a time when you have a momentary instance of faithlessness. Therefore, it is important to answer the question: how do we handle faith failures?

Even Paul, the great apostle, said, "The good that I would do, that I do not do. But that which I hate, I find myself doing (Romans 7:15 author's paraphrase)." In other words, Paul had to deal with faith failures. If Paul had faith failures, we can be sure we will also. So, we need to learn how to handle faith failures.

Challenge questions:
Have you had a faith failure since committing to Christ?
How did you handle the faith failure?

Causes of Faith Failures

What causes a faith failure? It is often the circumstances and situations in life that cause them. At other times it is the result of our experiences. For example, we know God to be a healer, but when we get sick in our body we begin to doubt if He's going to heal us. We worry thinking to ourselves, "I don't know when I'm going to get well." We become discouraged because it has taken so long. We forget the fact that God said He's a healer. We stop believing He will heal us. A faith failure is anytime we become doubtful of God's promises, have a momentary lapse concerning God's faithfulness, or moments of despair and unbelief. So, the question is: during such a time, when you're really going through and your life is falling apart because you can't see what God is doing, how do you handle it?

Abraham's Faith Failure

Abraham was on the mountain worshipping God. He built an altar at Bethel, in between Bethel and Ai, and he called on the Name of the Lord. God then promised to give him and his offspring the land of Canaan. This is a powerful promise because at the time Abraham and Sarah were childless. Yet, God made him this promise concerning his future children. Then a famine comes. We left Abraham worshipping, but now we meet him in famine.

Can you relate to Abraham's experience? Just last week everything was going okay in your life. Last week your body was doing just fine. You had a job last week. Last week it seemed like everything was finally lining up. But Saturday came or the phone rang and suddenly, your circumstances changed.

You went from a time of plenty to a time of not any.

If you have experienced something like that, then you know how Abraham felt. That's what a famine is. It is going from a time of abundance to a time of lack. Abraham and Sarah found themselves amid a famine; rich with God's promise, but in lack. They went from having all they needed to having nothing. They went from being blessed and highly favored to being in a state of absolute lack.

It seemed like just when God made the promise, circumstances changed. You may be going through that right now in your life. The circumstances in your life have changed and you're wondering what happened. You are trusting God, but now it seems that everything has fallen apart. God just told you He was going to bless and increase you so why are you in lack? Maybe you are wondering why God would let this happen to you. Why would God tell you He was going to bless you and then let famine come?

God had said to Abraham, "you're going to be the boss. In fact, Abraham, I'm going to bless you so abundantly that everybody all around the world is going to call you blessed." Then the famine came. He went from having plenty to not having any. I can imagine him thinking, "Wait a minute. God told me He was going to bless me, that my children were going to have this whole land. Why would He tell me that and then allow famine to come?"

Challenge question:
Can you relate to Abraham?

Perhaps that is how you feel at this moment. God told you what He was going to do. He showed you a revelation, a vision or a dream concerning what He was going to do in your life. Then during all of that, a famine came. Lack erupted. You had all you needed, but now you have nothing you need. Now you're wondering, "Why in the world would God let me go through this?"

Your circumstances are always either an opportunity to trust God or doubt God.

Whatever circumstance you are in, it's an opportunity to either stand and believe what God has told you, or to doubt and shrink back.

Abraham had a choice to make. He was in the land of promise. God promised him Canaan. He told Abraham, "I'm going to give you this land. And I'm going to bless you and bless you abundantly." Yet during a famine, Abraham decided, "I'm going to Egypt." Egypt wasn't the land God promised him. God had said nothing to him about that place.

Challenge question:
Do you find yourself in Egypt, living in a foreign place?

Maybe, you've made a decision because of an unexpected circumstance. Instead of trusting God in the land of promise, you've made a transition and took a detour back to the land where you once had provision. Let me explain. Abraham was already in the land of promise where God's presence was. He was already where God wanted him to be. Yet, because of the circumstances and situation, he decided on his own to go to Egypt. That was the faith failure.

"Now there was a famine in the land, and Abram went down to Egypt to live there for a while because the famine was severe (Genesis 12:10)."

Notice that there is no reference to Abraham, who had just finished worshipping, consulting God about what he should do now that the famine arose. It's almost as if he instantly forgot everything God had told him He was going to do. There are times during our faith journey when even though we have heard the promise of God when circumstances change, we decide to take matters back into our own hands.

Digest this spiritual truth: **You cannot do God's will your way!**

You and I have to learn that if God makes us a promise, it does not matter how long it takes, what we have to go through, what we have to give up, nor who leaves our life, we must stand until the promise comes to pass. Every time God makes a promise, He brings it to pass. Therefore, we must decide if we're going to wait on God or not. Abraham couldn't wait. He went to Egypt and as soon as he left for Egypt, the faith failure began.

Spiritual Principle: As soon as you leave the place of promise, the faith failure begins.

Complicating the Situation

Sarah was sixty-five at the time and Abraham was seventy-five. Not only was going to Egypt bad enough, Abraham thought to himself, "Sarah is so beautiful the men of Egypt will want her. She might be sixty-five, but she is still turning heads." I can imagine the conversation between Abraham and Sarah "because you're so fine we need to do something. I know God said, 'I'm going to bless those that bless you and curse those that curse you,' but the Egyptians weren't there when God spoke to me. They didn't hear God tell me He was going to bless me. They didn't hear God tell me He was going to curse those who cursed me. So, here's what I want us to do Sarah. Now, listen to me baby. You are so beautiful I want you to tell the Egyptians you are my sister so that they will spare my life." Then they set out for Egypt with their well-rehearsed plan. But there was a problem; God had already told Abraham, "You don't have to worry about anybody coming against you because if I'm on your side, I'll fight your battle." If Abraham had remembered that, perhaps, he would not have had Sarah lie.

Often, we put ourselves in bad situations because we forget God's promise and have a faith failure. We fail to believe God at His word, taking matters into our own hands. That is what Abraham did and that is what we do at times. Abraham complicated the situation by having Sarah lie. When we are in the midst of a faith failure, we must be careful not to make matters worse by trying to cover it up with dishonesty.

Faith Failures Are Not Fatal

It is important to know, even though a faith failure causes us to experience negative consequences, it is not fatal. You can and will survive! You might be in the midst of a faith failure right now. Perhaps you are in a place where you doubt everything God ever promised you. You may even find yourself amid Egypt when you should be in the Promised Land. The message for you is that your faith failure is not fatal. You will survive and be stronger because of it if you handle it the right way. Make this positive affirmation right now:

I'm going to live and not die!

Now believe it. Remember Satan is trying to use our faith failures to destroy us. He catches us when we're already feeling bad because we doubted and disobeyed God and tells us, "You're going to die. You will never get out of this one. Ha! You went down there to Egypt and now I'm going to kill you in Egypt." Satan is a liar! It is in these moments that we must remember that Satan does not have the power to kill. He can't do anything that God does not let him do in your life. So, if you keep on doing what God said do, even during your faith failure you will live.

The Power of Life and Death

In the midst of our faith failure we must remember that we still have the promise of God. The word of God tells us that the power of life and death are in the tongue (Proverbs 18:21). Abraham said that the Egyptians would find Sarah beautiful. While in Egypt, sure enough the Egyptians found her beautiful. He called it into existence. Often, we call our circumstances and situations into existence in our lives by what we say. When we doubt and disbelieve God and then speak negative things over our lives they often come to pass. Guard your words even when you are going through times of doubt. Because whatever you speak, you may speak into existence. You must understand the reason you're going through some of the things you're going through is because you have spoken them into existence. Stop speaking negativity over your life!

Spiritual Principle: Remember, you have the power of life and death in your tongue - speak life.

Our Faith Failure Impacts Others

News flash: your faith failure does not only have an impact on your life, but it also affects others. Pharaoh found himself in the midst of Abraham's faith failure. Pharaoh and his men suffered consequences because Abraham failed to trust God.

Families have been destroyed because of the faith failure of a family member generations ago. Some of our children, siblings, and spouses are dealing with the consequences of our faith failures. Don't let your faithlessness cause pain to those connected to you.

Abraham said, "Tell them you're my sister." Sarah said, "Okay, I'm your sister."

Then suddenly, Sarah was involved in Abraham's faith failure. Sarah became a slave in the harem of Pharaoh because Abraham doubted God and took matters into his own hands.

I have good news for those who may be experiencing a faith failure. Remember, God told Abraham "I'm going to bless those who bless you, and I'm going to curse those who curse you." It really didn't matter what Abraham did, because God didn't say, "If you do this, I'll do it." He made a unilateral covenant. It didn't matter how Abraham acted; God made a promise that He had to keep. Listen, God has made promises in our life, that it really doesn't matter how we act, He must keep them. In 2 Timothy 2:13 we read "If we are faithless, He remains faithful, for He cannot deny Himself." God's character is connected to His promises.

The only problem is that some of the promises that He keeps are going to wreak havoc in the lives of others and may destroy them if we don't believe. The people in our lives end up suffering when we don't believe God. Pharaoh, his men, his entire household became sick with serious diseases because Abraham failed to believe God. Abraham's faith failure was negatively impacting the Egyptians.

Challenge question:
How have your faith failures impacted others?

Pause to pray and reflect
This may be a time when you need to pause before going forward to go back to God, fall on your face before Him, and begin to repent and ask for forgiveness. You may even need to go back to some family members and some friends and ask them, "Please forgive me for my faith failure.

Blessed during a Faith Failure

Abraham went to Egypt because he had a faith failure, but he left Egypt blessed. God's grace and mercy are so awesome that He blesses us even in the middle of our mess-ups. He blesses us even when we are faithless. The Word declares "even if you're faithless, He will be faithful because He can't be faithless (2 Timothy 2:13)." God blesses us even when we blow it! Don't interpret this as a license to go out and do anything you want to do. Sin has consequences. You choose your actions, but you don't choose the consequences. It's not a license to sin. However, it should give us an assurance that even though we may experience a momentary faith failure—it's not fatal. God at times still blesses us even during our faith failure.

Removing Ourselves from the Place of Failure

Abraham realized he was out of position and outside of God's will. He had to leave Egypt. The first step in handling our faith failure to realize the impact it has on others. The second step is to remove ourselves from the place of our failure.

"Then Pharaoh gave orders about Abram to his men, and they sent him on his way, with his wife and everything he had (Genesis 12:20)."

"So Abram went up from Egypt to the Negev, with his wife and everything he had, and Lot went with him. Abram had become very wealthy in livestock and in silver and gold." (Genesis 13:1 and 2)

This teaches us what it means to remove ourselves from the place of our failure. Abraham packed up and reversed his steps. He went back to Canaan the place of the promise. We need to follow Abraham's example. Why? Because God's promise, presence, power, and provision are there. Everything you need is in the land of promise, not in the land of provision. Therefore, Abraham got up and he removed himself from the negative circumstances.

The length of our faith failure is determined by how quickly we come to our senses and remove ourselves from the place of failure. Our faith failures can last an instant, a minute, an hour, a day, a week, a year, ten years or even a lifetime. The faith failure doesn't stop until you remove yourself from the place of failure.

Challenge questions:
Are you in the midst of a faith failure?

If the answer is yes, these are the steps to take:

Recognize that you have had a faith failure.
Realize that it is affecting others.
Remove yourself from the place of your failure.

Pause and pray
Now is a good time to pause and pray. Ask God to show you what these steps look like for you in a practical way. Ask Him to show you what to do next. Listen for His answer.

Returning to the Presence of God through Worship

The last thing Abraham did was return to God's presence. This will be a recurring theme in Abraham's faith journey. It should also be a recurring theme in our journey to radical faith.

"From the Negev he went from place to place until he came to Bethel, to the place between Bethel and Ai where his tent had been earlier and where he had first built an altar. There Abram called on the name of the LORD (Genesis 13:3 and 4)."

If we are to overcome our faith failure and develop radical faith one of the most vital elements needed is intimacy with God. Intimacy with God is developed by spending time in His presence through worship. Worship is the most essential element in the life of the believer. Worship involves entering into the presence of God and communing with Him. It involves living in fellowship with God on a daily basis.

"God is spirit and they that worship Him must worship Him in spirit and in truth (John 4:24)."

Abraham returned to Bethel; this Hebrew word literally means the house of God. Beth=house and El=God. After leaving the place of his faith failure, Abraham returned to the presence of God. He renewed his relationship with God through worship. If you have suffered a faith failure and are ready to overcome it, why not take some time to repent and return to the presence of God through true worship.

I recommend a song by Matt Redman about true worship that is so powerful to me. It captures for me what worshiping God is really all about. In his song The Heart of Worship he sings about returning to the heart of God, bringing Him all that we are. My prayer is that we will return to true worship as we journey to radical faith, this is a good time to find that song and listen to it.

Letting Lot Go

I was born and raised in Nashville, Tennessee. After high school I moved to Memphis to attend college and graduate school. As I drew near the end of completing my master's degree, I felt led to return to Nashville to do my internship and then planned to move on. While in Nashville, I finally accepted my calling into ministry. After accepting the call, I knew my career path would change. For the next six years I remained in Nashville. I really did not have a clear picture of where the Lord was leading me. It was during this time that I experienced a major test of my faith. It was also during this time that I came face to face with the fact that God was changing my life path. I realized that as comfortable as I was in Nashville, God was leading me to leave. Nashville was my Lot. It was my place of familiarity. Yet God was clear, it was time for me to let Lot go. As you read on you will discover what I mean.

Moving on from Faith Failures

As we continue the journey toward radical faith, we turn our attention to Lot, Abraham's nephew. Genesis 13 contains the biblical account of Abraham and Lot parting company. We will use it to learn what it means to let Lot go.

"Now Lot, who was moving about with Abram, also had flocks and herds and tents. But the land could not support them while they stayed together, for their possessions were so great that they were not able to stay together. And quarreling arose between Abram's herdsmen and the herdsmen of Lot. The Canaanites and Perizzites were also living in the land at that time. So Abram said to Lot, "Let's not have any quarreling between you and me, or between your herdsmen and mine, for we are brothers. Is not the whole land before you? Let's part company. If you go to the left, I'll go to the right; if you go to the right, I'll go to the left." Lot looked up and saw that the whole plain of the Jordan was well watered, like the garden of the LORD, like the land of Egypt, toward Zoar. (This was before the LORD destroyed Sodom and Gomorrah.) So Lot chose for himself the whole plain of the Jordan and set out toward the east. The two men parted company: Abram lived in the land of Canaan, while Lot lived among the cities of the plain and pitched his tents near Sodom. Now the men of Sodom were wicked and were sinning greatly against the LORD. The LORD said to Abram after Lot had parted from him, "Lift up your eyes from where you are and look north and south, east and west. All the land that you see I will give to you and your offspring forever. I will make your offspring like the dust of the earth, so that if anyone could count the dust, then your offspring could be counted. Go, walk through the length and breadth of the land, for I am giving it to you." So Abram moved his tents and went to live near the great trees of Mamre at Hebron, where he built an altar to the LORD (Genesis 13:5-18)."

Saved for a Purpose

God is trying to get us to a place where we trust Him radically, to a place where even though we cannot see how He's moving, we don't understand why He's doing what He's doing, we believe Him and stand with Him, allowing Him to do in our lives what He wants to do. Some may call this blind trust. I call it complete trust.

As Christians, we know that our purpose has been defined by God. Therefore, when we begin our journey to radical faith, we do so with purpose. Please know that God has a purpose for your life. When you accepted Jesus as your Lord and Savior and were baptized, the reason why you were not taken out of the baptismal pool and snatched up to heaven immediately is that God has a purpose for you to fulfill in the earth. He wants to do something in you and through you that nobody else can do. Each of us has been designed and delivered by God so that He can use us to carry out His will on the earth. As we journey to radical faith, we are moving toward the purpose that God has for our lives. In order to accomplish what he assigned for us to do, we must come to a place where we recognize that anything, anybody, any place, or any habit that is hindering us from getting to God's purpose for us has to go. We must come to a place where we look around and we see all that God has promised us and raise the question, "What is keeping me from receiving the promises of God?"

Realizing the Lot in Our Lives

The account of Lot and Abraham is fascinating. Lot and Abraham both have many possessions. As a result, the land is not able to support both. It is when we realize that our purpose is being delayed because of something or someone to whom we are connected that identifies the "Lot" in our lives.

> **Lot represents that thing or that person in your life that is keeping you from getting to your place of purpose.**

It's the thing or the person that is keeping us from getting what God promised us. In John 10:10 Jesus declared that He came for His followers to have life "to the full". You may have been praying and asking, "God, when is it going to happen?" The answer may be as simple as, "As soon as you let Lot go." You may be waiting for God to deliver you out of a situation. You are tired of having to deal with the same habit. You are ready to be free once and for all. How do you get there? It begins with identifying your lot in life and letting it go.

Challenge questions:
What is hindering your progress toward your purpose?
Who is preventing you from moving forward in the things to which God has called you?

The Problem with Lot

When God called Abraham and gave him the promise, Lot was not mentioned. Yet as we follow Abraham's journey, Lot is with him. Lot, his herds and flocks are with Abraham and the land cannot support both (Genesis 13:6).

You may be wondering, what does all this have to do with radical faith and me? Lot was not there by divine design, but by the invitation of Abraham. Why did Abraham take Lot with him? Perhaps he felt obligated to him so took him along. Maybe there are people or things you are allowing to remain in your life out of obligation.

We will never get to the place of our purpose until we let Lot go.

We cannot experience radical faith until we get Lot out of our lives. Lot represents that which is not part of God's plan, purpose, and promise for you, but that you hold on to because it is comfortable and familiar. *Lot is a blessing-blocker.* As painful as it may be if Lot is in your life, you will never get the blessing God has for you. Lot is many things to many people. You may remember the saying, "That's my Lot in life." That statement was meant to describe a situation or circumstance in one's life that was beyond one's control. Yet there is no situation or circumstance in your life that is beyond God's control. God can set you free from whatever your *lot* is in life.

Defining Your Lot

The question has probably crossed your mind, what is my lot? It is important that we answer that question individually. Everyone's Lot is unique. However here are some examples of what a lot may be:

Relationships

Perhaps it is a relationship (friendship or romantic connection) that is not God's will. It does not mean that the person is bad or that the relationship is unhealthy. It is simply not what God intended for you. Any relationship that prevents you from receiving the promise, fulfilling God's purpose or trusting God radically it's a Lot.

Jobs/Career
For others your Lot may be your job or career. You desire to trust God radically and in fact want all that God has for you. However, your job has risen to the level that it is keeping you from going all out in pursuit of God. You find yourself focusing more of your time and energy on your job than you do on God. Your job is so important to you that you put the things of God on hold in order to fulfill your job obligations. Your Lot is your job.

You're so determined that you're going to stay on that job, you don't care what it costs you. You know that God told you it wasn't for you, yet you are still hanging on and you're wondering why you're not getting what God promised you. It's because you haven't let Lot go. Work is God-honoring, but it must not become our god!

Habits
Lot may be your habits, hang-ups, or things you must have. Anything you just will not do without. Alcohol and other addictions may be your lot. Any habit that hinders your commitment to Christ is Lot. It may be your need to please people instead of God. Positive or negative habits that are placed before God is Lot.

Pause and Pray: Ask God to reveal anything that is a Lot in your life.

Lot Hinders Your Progress

Abraham realized that Lot could not remain with him. He realized Lot was excess baggage. Abraham knew he could not move forward to receive what God promised him if Lot was with him.

Your divinely designed progress is hindered by excess baggage.

When you're carrying around people and things that God doesn't have for you, you can't really get into God's presence. Why not? Because—Lot represents your past. Lot represents what God told you to leave. Remember what God told Abraham? He said, "Now, here's what I want you to do. I want you to leave your country, leave your people, and leave your father's household and go to a land I will show you." God said, "leave it all behind!"

Has God told you to leave some people or things? If you haven't, you are trying to move forward while looking backward. Perhaps, you remember the good times or even the bad times from the past. You cannot get to the place of your purpose if Lot is in your life because you're still connected to the past. God wants us to be free to receive the purpose and the promise He has for us. The radical faith to which God is calling us requires us to let Lot go. We have to be willing to say, "I love you, but you represent a place where God told me to leave. I'm sorry, but we have to part company because you're the past and I'm moving toward the future. You're good and all of that and I really feel good when I take you in, but I've got to let you go because I'm trying to get somewhere and the only way I'll get there is if I part with Lot. So as of today, I'm letting Lot go."

It's Important to Recognize When It's Time to Part Company

The land could not support both Abraham and Lot, so an argument broke out. Imagine the herdsmen of Lot and Abraham were out there on the plain as the cattle were eating the grass. Then suddenly Abraham's men looked up and said, "Wait a minute. You all are not supposed to be here anyway. You were not the ones who received the promise. Our master received the promise. Why don't you go?" Then, Lot's herdsmen said, "Listen, we've been with him the whole time. We belong to his nephew and this is our land just like it's your land." They started arguing with one another.

The lesson in this conflict is: you must recognize when it's time to part company.

Abraham had to come to grips with the fact that it was time to move on. He was the recipient of the divine promise, but Lot was blessed by being close to him. Lot was getting blessings through Abraham. Don't get upset, but there may be people around you that God never connected to you that are getting blessed by being near you. Lot was blessed simply by being with Abraham.

Spiritual Principle: Don't let Lot enjoy the blessings God intends for you!

Abraham was receiving what God had for him, but Lot was over there going, "Oh, glory, God! Hallelujah!" He was so excited. Do you know why? Because he was getting blessings. He was increasing right alongside Abraham. There are people today that are increasing right alongside of you because they're getting blessings God designed for you.

The other thing it is important to see is that when the strife broke out, it was because there was a point of saturation reached. Abraham had been blessed so much and Lot was just as blessed because he was with him. They both were full of the blessings of the Lord. They were so blessed that the land could no longer support them. There comes the point when the land of our life can no longer handle the abundance of our increase and the increase of Lot. It is then that it is time to let Lot go. God wants you to know that Lot is that thing that keeps you from moving forward to your purpose.

Challenge questions:
What is your Lot?
Who is your Lot?

Identify the place of saturation. Identify the area of your life that can no longer handle you and Lot.

Now It's Time to Let Go

Once you recognize the need to part company, follow Abraham's lead (Genesis 13:9). He said, "Okay, here's the deal we have to part company. I'm sorry."

Maybe this personal testimony will help this make more sense to you.

> In 2004 I found myself having a conversation with my boss. I had become the second in charge of a multimillion-dollar non-profit organization. I shared with him that I was getting to the place where I knew I could not continue to work there and do what God wanted me to do. I was getting to the place where I recognized that because God had called us to full-time ministry. I shared that God didn't call me to pastor while working 40-plus hours on a job. So, I sat down, and I talked with my boss. My boss said, "I want you to know you have my blessing. I want you to know anything I can do to help." By the end of the year the organization I was working for merged with another organization and my position was eliminated. I asked God what I should do. Should I pursue a position with the new entity? God said to me, "It's time to let Lot go."

What am I saying? What does that have to do with radical faith? Ask yourself, where's my faith? Do I trust God enough to step out on faith and let Lot go?

Many times, we hold on to Lot because it's a crutch. A crutch can't get you to the place of your purpose. You may be holding on to people, places or things because you are afraid to let Lot go. That is what I faced in 2004. Please know, you can't get your blessing until you let Lot go. Tell your Lot, "We have to separate!" God's trying to take me somewhere and I refuse to be hindered. I want my purpose. I want to get what God has for me."

God may be stirring up in you the desire and resolve to get what He has for you. If you want it, then you must be willing to let Lot go in order to get to the place of your purpose. Make up your mind to let Lot go. It's time to have the conversation, cancel the subscription, and/or turn in your notice. It's time to let Lot go! God has promised to bless and increase you and the only way to receive it is to let Lot go!

The Grass is not Always Greener

Lot had been with Abraham for quite a while. I would argue he had witnessed Abraham's faith. Yet his story, throughout scripture, does not indicate he internalized his uncle's faith.

Genesis 13:10 states *"Lot looked up and saw that the whole plain of the Jordan was well watered."*

The conversation between Lot and Abraham may have gone something like this: "Look, Lot. Here's the deal. It's time to separate. Here's the whole land. I'm going to let you choose first. You can take the right and I'll take the left. If you decide to take the left, I'll take the right. Whatever you want, Lot, it's yours."

Lot's first crucial mistake was that he looked with his own eyes. He did not rely on God's providence and provision. "Lot looked up." There's no mention that Lot prayed to God. There's no mention that Lot consulted God. He simply surveyed the land and said, "This place looks good. I'll go there."

Here's a warning; everything that looks good isn't good.

Just because it looks like it's green does not mean it is. The grass is not always greener on the other side. I have heard it said that everything that looks good to you is not good for you. If Lot had taken the time to pray and consult God, he could have been blessed. As it turns out, he moved to Sodom, fertile land with corrupt people.

Challenge questions:
Do you find yourself in sinful surroundings?
Are you in a place of utter degradation because you happened to assess things on your own instead of trusting God?
Did you rely on your own ability to decide instead of relying on God's ability to direct you?
Are you now in a place of absolute darkness?

Perhaps you're living in hell on earth because instead of trusting God, you trusted yourself. Lot found himself in a place where the men hated God because he did not rely on God. When we wait on God to bless us and stop doing things on our own, our blessing will be magnified.

Don't end up in a place of darkness because you fail to consult God!

God Wants You to See Your Place of Blessing
When Abraham and Lot parted company, "The LORD said to Abram after Lot had parted from him, "Lift up your eyes from where you are and look north and south, east and west. All the land that you see I will give to you and your offspring forever (Genesis 13:14-15)."

As we journey to radical faith, we must remember God is the provider of the promise and the purpose. This is crucial because, when we finally let Lot go, it is then God steps in to bring the promise to fulfillment. That's when God steps in to move us to the place of our purpose. If you are to get there, here are three practical actions God wants you to take.

Look Up

He says, "Lift your eyes up. Look up." As you are reading this God is saying, "Look up. Things may be going bad in your life. You may be looking down because of all that is happening. You may be constantly depressed because you are going through repeatedly," but God is saying to you today, "Look up, trust Me and I will bless you. Rely on Me and the blessings will be so greatly increased that you will not even have room enough to receive them."

Get Up

Then God said to Abraham, "All the land that you see I will give to you and your offspring forever. I will make your offspring like the dust of the earth, so that if anyone could count the dust, then your offspring could be counted. Go, walk (Genesis 13:15)." After He tells us to look up, God says get up. Stop wallowing in your situation. Stop laying down in your circumstances and get up to go to your purpose. Stop being stagnant in your condition and get up because God said, "I told you I will do this. Now get up!" There's someone reading this and God's word to you is, "Get up!" You've been wallowing in self-pity long enough. God is saying, "Get up. I've given you a promise and I'm ready to bring your promise to completion. So, get up and start walking." Get up and go get what God has promised you.

Go Up
After Abraham got up and walked around the land, God said "come up into My presence." Even as you are reading this God is inviting you to go up into His presence. This would be a good time to begin praising God. Abraham began to praise God.

"So Abram moved his tents and went to live near the great trees of Mamre at Hebron, where he built an altar to the LORD."

Abraham built an altar. The purpose of the altar is worship. You do not build an altar for beauty. You build an altar because you intend to use it to get into the presence of God. After you let Lot go, after you look up and get up, it's time to go up into God's presence in worship!

A Prayer of Release
It's time to let Lot go. I encourage you to pray this prayer of release in faith as you let Lot go. "God, today, I know that _____ (whatever person, habit, mindset, practice, belief etc.), has been my Lot. Today I release Lot to You. I look up, changing my perspective. I get up, changing my posture. I go up, changing my position. I trust you to release me from Lot and Lot from me. In Jesus' name. Amen"

Preparing for the Blessing

"One who had escaped came and reported this to Abram the Hebrew. Now Abram was living near the great trees of Mamre the Amorite, a brother of Eshcol and Aner, all of whom were allied with Abram. When Abram heard that his relative had been taken captive, he called out the 318 trained men born in his household and went in pursuit as far as Dan. During the night Abram divided his men to attack them and he routed them, pursuing them as far as Hobah, north of Damascus. He recovered all the goods and brought back his relative Lot and his possessions, together with the women and the other people. After Abram returned from defeating Kedorlaomer and the kings allied with him, the king of Sodom came out to meet him in the Valley of Shaveh (that is, the King's Valley). Then Melchizedek king of Salem brought out bread and wine. He was priest of God Most High, and he blessed Abram, saying, "Blessed be Abram by God Most High, Creator of heaven and earth. And blessed be God Most High, who delivered your enemies into your hand." Then Abram gave him a tenth of everything. The king of Sodom said to Abram, "Give me the people and keep the goods for yourself." But Abram said to the king of Sodom, 'I have raised my hand to the LORD, God

Most High, Creator of heaven and earth, and have taken an oath that I will accept nothing belonging to you, not even a thread or the thong of a sandal, so that you will never be able to say, 'I made Abram rich.' I will accept nothing but what my men have eaten and the share that belongs to the men who went with me-to Aner, Eshcol and Mamre. Let them have their share (Genesis 14:13-24)."

Radical Faith Produces True Deliverance—One Woman's Story

Carrie was addicted to drugs for many years. It left her homeless, broken, and in poor health. Her relationship with her children was negatively impacted by her addiction. She came to one of our Living Life Free Addiction Deliverance meetings one evening and God spoke through me to tell her "She was not waiting on God to set her free, He was waiting on her." She believed and received that word and that very night she was set free. Carrie has now been free for over ten years. Just as God set Carrie free because of her faith in Him, He can set anyone free who will trust Him radically.

Faith that Has Substance

The faith we're moving toward is not empty. It is filled with God's amazing promises. When Abraham left Haran, he wasn't traveling without a promise. He left believing the promise God gave him. The faith God has called us to causes us to move past our comfort zone and that which is commonly accepted as religion. It is a faith, based on God's amazing promises. It is these promises that are the substance of radical faith. Because of that, He's asked us to move to a place where we trust Him completely. That's radical faith!

Radical faith says, *"I don't care what it costs me, I don't care what I have to give up, I don't care who has to leave my life, I don't care where I have to go, where I have to live, I'll live in a shoebox if it's where I know God told me to live because I want to be blessed by Him."*

In Hebrews 11:1 we read, "Now faith is the substance of things hoped for, the evidence of things not seen." Our faith has substance to it. It may not be visible, but it is real! That's good news today. Here are just a few things God promises us:

To those in need of a friend:
He'll be a friend that sticks closer than your brother.

To those who are parentless:
He'll be your father and your mother at the same time in the way that He loves you.

To those who feel defeated:
He promised that He would make you more than conquerors through Christ Jesus.

To those in need:
He promised He would meet all your needs.

Matthew 6:33 states, "But seek first His Kingdom and His righteousness, and all these things will be added to you." WOW! That's a promise. God doesn't call us to trust Him without providing us something of substance to hold on to. He gives us faith with substance!

Radical faith has substance!

The Lie of Insufficiency

At times, we as followers of Christ believe the lies of the enemy. One of those lies goes something like this, we must trust God, have a relationship with God and live to please God and we get nothing in return. It sounds like this when people believe it: "I have to give up everything, I can't hold on to anything. I have to quit drinking, smoking, lying, and everything else to follow Jesus." But the truth is, you don't have to give any of those things up. You simply have to say yes in faith and start pursuing God. When one starts pursuing God with a radical faith, He will give you a new heart and mind so that you know longer desire those things.

The lie says I can't, I'm not able to quit, I can't give it up. That is the lie of insufficiency. Radical faith says, I know God can do it in me. Radical faith in the substance of God's promise positions you to experience freedom in Christ!

Learning to Actively Wait

All of us enjoy hearing testimonies like Carrie's, yet that is not everyone's experience. It was not Abraham's experience. He left Haran expecting God to fulfill the promise immediately. He was like many of us; eagerly expecting immediate manifestation. I can hear Abraham now, "I'm glad for the promises, I thank God that He's made them, I know I'm going to be blessed and I am called to be a blessing to others. Yet, it's the waiting that I have a hard time enduring."

Challenge questions:
Do you ever get tired of waiting on the promises of God to come to pass?
Does it get hard at times to keep waiting in faith?

If you answered yes, then let me share something that will help you. We are not called to wait idly for God to fulfill His promises. Many times, we prolong the manifestation of the promise because we wait idly for God to bring it to pass. So often we have the mindset "God, go ahead and do what you're going to do. Move when you're ready. I'll just wait here Lord." If that is your mindset, here's God's word to you, "begin making preparations and while you're waiting, busy yourself serving." Let's find help from Abraham's life to know what to do while waiting for God to give us what He's promised us. Let's learn from Abraham how to actively wait.

Unexpected Situations

We all face unexpected situations when we decide to live for God. Following God is a risky undertaking.

Challenge questions:
Have you found it necessary to let Lot go?
Are you ready to move to where God wants you to be?
Are you listening carefully to God's instructions?

Abraham was finally ready to prepare for the promise. He had moved past his faith failure. He had let Lot go. Yet, while he's in the midst of preparation, he gets a message. Listen carefully, there will be times when you will be in the midst of preparing to get what God has for you; when you will be doing exactly what God said to do. You will be preparing for your blessing. When suddenly you will receive a message that something is not right. That's exactly what happened to Abraham (Genesis 14:13-24). As Abraham prepared to receive what God had for him, suddenly a messenger came and told him his nephew had been taken captive.

> **On this journey to radical faith, we will encounter unexpected situations!**

It seems he told Abraham that with an expectation that he would do something about it. When Abraham heard this he didn't say, "God told me to let Lot go, so that's the end of it. Lot's out of my life. I've moved on."

Let me make a clarifying statement. When your "Lot" is a person, letting them go doesn't mean you give up on them coming into a relationship with God or that you turn your back on them spiritually. It means that you make the decision not to let them hinder your progress. It means not letting them keep you from getting where God is taking you. You are still willing to reach back to help them if they are willing. That's what Abraham did (Genesis 14:13-16). He let Lot go, but he reached back when he was in trouble to help him.

> **Possessing the promises of God does not prevent us from reaching back to save others!**

God has called us to relationship with others. We cannot forget that we are inextricably bound to one another. Dr. Martin Luther King, Jr., said it like this, "There can be freedom for none until there is freedom for all." God is relational. He created us for relationship with others. If we are truly followers of God, we must know how to be relational. We cannot be deceived into believing that moving in faith toward our promise is a reason to neglect others in need.

What does this look like?

It looked like for me for a number of years each Wednesday night, whether I felt like it or not, getting in my Jeep, usually about 6:40, to head to 28th and North Avenue. There I would spend time with a group of fourteen men in a residential treatment program. Some of them were saved and some were not. Some of them could care less if we came every week and some of them wanted us to be there. But it really didn't matter because we were going there to minister the Word with the hope that one of them might get saved; that one of them might get it and get into relationship with God.

That is a picture of moving to radical faith while reaching back to save others.

How can we move to the place of our promise and get what God has for us if we won't reach back? We must be willing to deal with the unexpected situations that require us to reach back to rescue others while we are preparing to go to the place of our promise.

> **They are not a distraction; they are part of your preparation.**

Growing up I remember hearing a song with these lyrics:

"Heaven is my goal. Each and every day. I've got to keep on moving, moving in the right way. If I stumble, while I'm on my way; step aside, don't you block my way. I don't want nobody *always stumbling over me."* (Dr. Charles G. Hayes and the Cosmopolitan Church of Prayer, 1979).

The message is simple. While I am pursuing a relationship with God and moving toward radical faith, I cannot be so single-minded and forward focused that I forget about my brother who is hurting; my sister who is going through. God says it like this through Paul, *"Brothers, if someone is caught in a sin, you who are spiritual should restore him gently (Galatians 6:1)."*

The Need for Trained Spiritual Soldiers

Three hundred eighteen; that's the number of trained men, Abraham assembled to go with him to rescue Lot and his family. Abraham did not take house servants with him to save Lot and the others. He didn't go get the weekend warriors or Sunday saints. He recognized, "this is war!" When you're going into war, you need trained fighters.

Whether you realize it or not, we are in the midst of spiritual warfare. The devil is wreaking havoc in the earth realm and God is looking for believers who are willing to go into strict training, who are willing to go into hand-to-hand combat so that they can reach back and rescue those who are lost. **You must get trained.** As we journey to radical faith, we are on a mission to reach back and save the lost.

Jesus, when giving the mission statement for His ministry said it like this,

"The Spirit of the LORD is on me, because He has anointed me to proclaim good news to the poor. He has sent me to bind up the brokenhearted, to proclaim freedom for the prisoners and

recovery of sight for the blind, to set the oppressed free, to proclaim the year of the Lord's favor." (Luke 4:18-19).

He understood that His whole ministry was to reach out to the helpless, the hopeless, and the hurting; to go get those in captivity and set them free. He understood that His assignment was to bring them into a place where they could walk in liberty and relationship with God. That is our mission as Christ-followers as well.

Knowing there was a need to rescue Lot, Abraham went into battle with the goal of victory. We are fighting with victory as the goal. Losing is not an option. We are on the winning team! Let's go into the streets and alleys to rescue those God has called us to save.

The Blessings Come After the Fight

"After Abram returned from defeating Kedorlaomer and the kings allied with him (Genesis 14:17)."

So many people want the blessings of the Lord, but they do not want to go through the battle to receive them. However, we receive our blessings after we've fought the battle. It was after Abraham returned that the King of Sodom and the King of Salem, Melchizedek, the High Priest, came out to bless him.

"Blessed be Abram by God Most High (Genesis 14:19)."

Many people want the blessings before the battle, the medal before running the race, and the belt without winning the fight. But the blessing comes after the fight.

Melchizedek blessed Abraham after he rescued Lot. Victory comes after the battle! I'll prove it from the Word:

"Do you not know that in a race all the runners run, but only one gets the prize? Run in such a way as to get the prize. Everyone who competes in the games goes into strict training. They do it to get a crown that will not last; but we do it to get a crown that will last forever. Therefore, I do not run like a man running aimlessly; I do not fight like a man beating the air. No, I beat my body and make it my slave so that after I have preached to others, I myself will not be disqualified for the prize (1 Corinthians 9:24-27)."

Paul is saying, "Don't you know, if you're going to get the blessings, you have to go into battle. You must fight first. You must stand up against the enemy in order to win.
The Old Testament is filled with images of Israel, God's people, going into physical battle in order to possess the promise. The New Testament is filled with God's people, the Church, going into spiritual battle in order to possess the promise.

Radical faith equips us to stand up and fight!

It's important to realize it's not really a fight at all. The truth of the matter is the battle has already been fought in the spiritual realm. We are fighting a defeated foe.

We're not fighting for victory we're fighting **from** victory.

The Word says this is true!

"For we are more than conquerors through Christ Jesus our Lord." Romans 8:37

"No weapon formed against us shall prosper." Isaiah 54:17

"The weapons of our warfare have divine power to demolish strongholds." 2 Corinthians 10:4

"Submit therefore to God. Resist the devil and he has to flee!" James 4:7

"the accuser of our brethren has been thrown down..." Revelation 12:10

You've already been guaranteed victory. You're already a winner. All you must do is show up with your armor on, with your sword in your hand, and say, "Okay, Lord, I'm reporting for duty." As soon as you report, the Spirit inside of you rises up and begins to use the weapons of your warfare to become your strong and mighty arm to lead you into victory. The reason you're losing is that you won't fight. If you fight, you will win every time. God is raising up an army of trained soldiers with radical faith to fight against the schemes of the enemy.

Take up your weapons and fight!

Two Principles Concerning Spiritual Blessings

When we understand our blessings, obedience is not a burden.

"And blessed be God Most High, who delivered your enemies into your hand (Genesis 14:20)."

Melchizedek, King of Salem spoke these words to Abraham.

"Then Abram gave him a tenth of everything."

Now see the words of verses 18-20 together: *"Then Melchizedek king of Salem brought out bread and wine. He was priest of God Most High, and he blessed Abram, saying, 'Blessed be Abram by God Most High, Creator of heaven and earth. And blessed be God Most High, who delivered your enemies into your hand.' Then Abram gave him a tenth of everything."*

All blessings are given by God. God is committed to blessing us both physically and spiritually. People are not the source of our blessings. Although Melchizedek gave Abraham the bread and wine, it was God who blessed him. God blessed Abraham through Melchizedek. God uses people to release blessings, but it's not the person blessing you, it's God blessing you through the person. You are blessed through people not by people!

How did Abraham respond to receiving the blessing? He took a tenth of all he gained and gave it to Melchizedek, the High Priest. Nobody prompted him to give. Melchizedek didn't quote "Bring the whole tithe into the storehouse, that there may be food in my house. Test me in this," says the LORD Almighty, "and see if I will not throw open the floodgates of heaven and pour out so much blessing.... (Malachi 3:10)" to Abraham. Abraham recognized God had blessed him through Melchizedek and gave freely.

When we fully understand how blessed we are by God obedience in every area of our lives will be much easier.

Getting ready to get blessed requires us to understand that God is the source of our blessing and then act in obedience to Him. Abraham gave a tenth of all he gained. Abraham's faith prompted him to give. Radical faith prompts us to give freely and generously unto God.

Challenge question:
Will you freely give to God out of all that you have knowing He is the source of your blessing?

Melchizedek, God's appointed instrument, blessed Abraham. In response, Abraham sowed the tithe into him. Then the king of Sodom says (I'm paraphrasing), "Now, Abram, I know that you're really blessed, so here's what I want you to do. I want you to take all the goods and just give me the people back. You can have everything; I'll give it all to you." If we are honest, most of us would have been holding your hands out and saying, "Give it here. Give it all here." But there was a problem with that because God was the one who blessed him and made the promise. If Abraham took the goods from the King of Sodom, he would have accepted counterfeit blessings.

Remember the source of your blessings is God, not people.

Abraham showed no confusion about the source of his blessings. "But Abram said to the king of Sodom, "I have raised my hand to the LORD, God Most High, Creator of heaven and earth, and have taken an oath that I will accept nothing belonging to you, not even a thread or the thong of a sandal, so that you will never be able to say, 'I made Abram rich (Genesis 14:22)'" Many times we fail to understand this spiritual principle and accept counterfeit blessings. There are many Christians bragging on counterfeit blessings.

What is a counterfeit blessing? Any blessing received in the wrong way, with the wrong motive, or from the wrong source, is a counterfeit blessing. If you have to compromise your convictions or integrity to receive it, if the person offering it is doing so in order to gain access to you in an unhealthy way, or if the blessing comes with strings attached, it's counterfeit. When we accept counterfeit blessings, Satan has us in his hip pocket. He has deceived us into believing we can receive blessings contrary to the will of God, and it is still from God.

If it doesn't come to you the way God said it would

If it doesn't come the way God promised it

It's not from God.

You can't let everybody sow seeds into your life. I am convinced if Abraham had accepted these blessings, he would have moved outside of God's will. Not necessarily cutting off the promise but prolonging its manifestation.

Challenge questions:
Are you experiencing a delay in the manifestation of what God promised?
Are counter blessings clogging the way so that the real blessings are being delayed?

It may be time to get rid of some things that didn't come from God. If God promised it, He's the only One who can bring it to pass. When God brings it to pass, you'll never have to question is it really from God. Abraham said (paraphrasing), "You have lost your mind. If I take this thing from you, you'll be able to declare, 'I made Abram rich.'"

There are some people who want to be able to declare, "I made you who you are. I made you." That's the reason you must be careful who you let give you things because instead of giving God the glory, they'll want the glory. If we are to receive the blessing of God as promised, we must not let other people take God's glory. We have to have the mindset that the Apostle Paul had when he wrote; *"I know whom I have believed, and I am persuaded that He is able to keep that which I've committed to Him against that day (2 Timothy 2:12)."* What was Paul saying? "I won't take counterfeit blessings. What God has for me is for me. I'm convinced that He can keep that which I've committed to Him until the appointed day. Whatever I must go through, however long I must wait, however much preparation I must to do, I'll do it because when the blessings come it will be worth it."

It's Time to Get Ready to Get Our Blessings

Challenge questions:
Are you getting ready to get blessed?
Have you made up your mind that you will wait as long as it takes?
Are you willing to part with counterfeit blessings in order to make room for the real ones?
Will you obey God freely, understanding the blessings are worth it?

Radical faith prepares us for the blessings God has for us!

A Prayer of Confession and Commitment:

Oh, God, I'm waiting on You. You have made me promises. You told me You were going to pour out blessings. You told me You'd bless me abundantly. You told me You'd give me life and life more abundantly. Now, God, I'm in the preparation process and I'm ready to receive the blessings. Whenever You're ready, God. I'm working while I'm waiting. I refuse to stop working. When the blessings come, God, I'll be ready. Bring on the blessings. Open up the windows of heaven and pour out the blessings you have promised me! In the name of Jesus, Amen!

It's time to get ready to get blessed!

God said it.
That settles it.
Now what?

Learning to Not Be Moved by What You See

As I sit to write this, I just ended a call with one of our longtime members who has decided to leave the church. I'm sure he has very good reasons and yet it hinders what we are believing God to do. We are believing God to grow our ministry to be one that looks like heaven and impacts our community in a tangible way. In fact, God has been clear that He wants us to make a huge difference in our community and in the city. How are we supposed to do that when people continue to leave the church at the same rate as people coming into the church? From a visual perspective this seems like an impossible task, however from a spiritual perspective it is entirely possible. How so you may ask? Simply stated— because God said it and that settles it. Therefore, I don't let the physical shape the spiritual. I let the spiritual determine what's going to happen in the physical realm. Amen. How? By exercising radical faith to trust what is unseen not what is seen (Hebrews 11:3).

If we are to operate in radical faith, we must not let what we see change what we know. I've learned not to let the physical; what I can see, touch, taste, smell, and hear, shape the spiritual; what I know is going on in the spiritual realm. This has been true throughout my spiritual journey and it is even truer today. Perhaps in your life you look around at the natural circumstances that you see and think there is no way you will ever be, do, or have what God has promised you. If that is the case, I want to encourage you to stop believing what you see. Stop letting your natural determine your spiritual. Look not with the eyes of flesh, but with the eyes of the spirit. God wants to get to you to the point where you trust Him radically, where you believe what He has said even though you can't see it. God wants to get you to the place where you declare God said it, that settles it!

Standing on God's Word

"After this, the word of the LORD came to Abram in a vision: 'Do not be afraid, Abram. I am your shield, your very great reward.' But Abram said, "O Sovereign LORD, what can you give me since I remain childless and the one who will inherit my estate is Eliezer of Damascus?" And Abram said, "You have given me no children; so a servant in my household will be my heir." Then the word of the LORD came to him: "This man will not be your heir, but a son coming from your own body will be your heir." He took him outside and said, "Look up at the heavens and count the stars if indeed you can count them." Then he said to him, "So shall your offspring be." Abram believed the LORD, and he credited it to him as righteousness (Genesis 15:1-6)."

When God says something, that's the end of the discussion, we are to just wait for it to manifest. We're to do everything we need to do until it happens, but we are to stand confidently assured that it will happen. *Abraham believed God and it was credited to him as righteousness.* Abraham was an incredibly faith-filled man! Think about it—at the voice of God he left all that was familiar to him and began a journey to an undisclosed location. Can't you hear the conversation now between him and Sarah?

Abraham: "Honey, honey, get up. We must go. Let's go. We have to move."

Sarah: "Well, where are we going?"

Abraham: "I don't know. But I know God says it's time to go. We must go. We have somewhere to be."

Sarah: "What do you mean, Abram, God said it's time to go? What are you talking about?"

Abraham: "Honey, I don't understand. I'm not sure. He just told me to leave everything. He said to leave my family and leave my father's house and leave everything and go."

Sarah: "Abram, are you sure?"

Abraham: "Listen, baby, I don't have time for the discussion now. I don't have time to explain anymore. God said it, that settles it, now I have to go."

That's the type of faith God wants us to have. He wants us to get to the place that when God says it, that settles it, and then we go. That is called standing on God's word.

Radical faith is standing on God's word even when it doesn't make sense!

Handling the Now What

Imagine with me what Abraham's relatives must have said when he told them he was leaving. "Abraham, what are you talking about? You're going somewhere and you don't know where you're going? What do you mean? Don't you know that there are thieves out there? Abraham, come on, you have lost your mind. What about everything you have here?" I can hear Abraham saying, "You know what, I don't know. I don't know where I'm going. I won't even know until I get there. But God said it, that settles it, and now I have to go." When we are called to radical faith we declare, "God said, that settles it!" Then we find ourselves saying, "Now what, God?"

It is difficult to handle the now what after we step out in faith. I remember the first time one of our founding families decided to all leave the church all at the same time. The Lord was starting to do some amazing things. We were growing and the power of God was moving. We made a decision they didn't like, and they all left. I found myself saying to God through tears, "Now what." Anyone who has ever stepped out in radical faith has had 'now what' moments. Now what moments are those times when you cannot move forward until you receive a clear word from God. Never ignore a now what moment!

Challenge questions:
Are you at a place of now what on your journey to radical faith?

Have you reached a place where you can't move forward without hearing from God concerning what's next? If you are at a place of now what, trust God for giving you the answer you need to move forward in radical faith.

We all experience now what moments when we are called to radical faith

Reaching the Place of Your Now What

After Abraham rescues Lot, he is left alone with his thoughts. It is often when we are left alone with our thoughts, that we have our now what moments. It is when we have done all that we know to do and yet still do not have what God promised us, that we arrive at our now what moment. Imagine Abraham saying, *"This is it? I can't go any farther. I've gone as far as I can go. Until I hear the voice of God, I will not travel any farther."* This was Abraham's now what moment. He said, "I don't know what I'm supposed to do next." You may find yourself at the place of your now what. Maybe you are saying to yourself, "I won't take another step in my life, I won't make another decision, I won't do anything else until I hear the voice of God." If so good. That's exactly where God wants you to be.

I'm convinced Abraham was at his now what moment. What did he do? He built an altar. Perhaps he thought to himself: "Maybe if I lay prostrate in His presence. Maybe if I bow down and worship Him, maybe if I cry out to Him, He'll respond and tell me where I'm supposed to go." I've learned, when you worship God, that's when the Word comes. Often, we can't hear the Word because we will not move ourselves to a place of worship. We will not lay prostrate before the throne of the Most High God until He speaks to us.

In the place of now what, lay before the Lord until He speaks

God Responds to Our Now What Moments

As Abraham worshiped, God spoke. He said, "Abraham, to you and all your kindred, all your offspring, I'm giving this land." God provided Abraham the answer he needed. When we are in our now what moments, God will provide us the answers we need.

We simply need to get into His presence. There is a pattern revealed in Genesis 15:1-6 that we should take note of: every time you need to hear from God, you need to get into His presence.

Bethel in Hebrew means "house of God." During his journey toward radical faith Abraham constantly went back to God's house. On this occasion God said to you and your offspring, "I am giving this land." This is the second time now God has made this promise to Abraham. Yet it's almost as if Abraham wasn't hearing God. Perhaps you are saying to yourself Abraham believed God and left everything, surely, he must have heard God. There was a problem with God's promise: Abraham didn't have any children. He and Sarah were childless. She was barren. Yet God kept saying to him over and over again, "To you and your offspring I am giving this land. I'll make you a great nation. I'll bless you." It was like Abraham was walking around in a daze. He was mesmerized by the majestic melody of God's voice or something and he wasn't getting it. Why would I say that? Because He never said anything. He never questioned God. It seems that Abraham said "God said it, that settles it.

Don't Be Mesmerized and Miss the Message

At times we miss the message God has for us because we get so mesmerized by God's voice. We exclaim "Oh wow, God spoke to me!" We get so caught up in the fact that God, the Creator of the universe, would take time to speak to us that we miss what He's saying. It's like Abraham didn't even hear what God was saying, all he knew was God spoke to him.

We must make sure we get the message.

Finally, Abraham is now in a place where he is getting ready for the blessing. He has let Lot go, dealt with his faith failure and is getting ready to get blessed. At that point "the word of the LORD came to Abram in a vision." God tells Abraham "Do not be afraid, Abram. I am your shield, your very great reward." Then suddenly, a light bulb went on, the wax popped out of his ears, and he heard what God was saying. Abraham remembered every word that God had said to him. Abraham said "Wait a minute. What do you mean, 'Do not be afraid? I am your shield, your very great reward'? What do you mean you're going to bless me, and this land is going to belong to me and my offspring?" All the promises suddenly rushed back to his remembrance, and he said, "O Sovereign LORD, what can you give me since I remain childless and the one who will inherit my estate is Eliezer of Damascus?" "Oh, God, what do you mean you're going to bless me? Oh, God, what do you mean you're going to make me a great nation? Oh, God, what do you mean you're my shield and my very great reward? Don't you see the condition that I'm in? Don't you realize that Sarai's womb is bound up like a closed dam? Don't you realize that we're childless and there's no seed to share my inheritance with?" In Hebrew culture, the child represented the seed. If there was no child, there was no seed. If there was no seed, you were not blessed, you were cursed. Abraham said, "God, I hear you. I've heard everything you've ever said to me, but somehow it doesn't line up with my current condition."

Challenge questions:
Has God made promises to you that don't fit your current condition?
Are you struggling to believe God because of what you are currently experiencing?

I want to let you know you are in good company. The father of faith struggled to believe God's promise also. Abraham says to God "You're talking about giving an inheritance to my offspring. Don't you know the only offspring I have is a slave?" Finally, Abraham stopped listening to the melody of God's voice and started hearing the message God spoke.

It's time to stop listening to the melody of God's voice and start hearing the message He is speaking!

Hearing God's Message May Produce Doubt

News flash—when you finally hear God's message, it may produce doubt.

When Abraham finally heard God's words, doubt set in. One of the ways Satan infiltrates the Church is by attacking us when we doubt. He gets us to think that if we're truly saved and filled with the Holy Spirit, we will not have any doubts.

He wants us to believe that if you doubt, you must not really love God. One lie of the enemy is if you doubt, you are not praying enough, or you need to fast more often. Maybe he tells you if you're doubting, you must be involved in sin. Yet throughout scripture we see people of God struggle with doubt. You are in good company—Moses doubted, Gideon doubted, Esther doubted. Abraham doubted. He had faith, but he didn't see how God was going to bless him when he had no children. You may be filled with all kinds of doubt as you pursue radical faith. I want you to know that's exactly where God wants you to be right now.

You can't get your blessing until you deal with your doubt

I can imagine Abraham's conversation with God "God, you've been making all these promises. You've been telling me all these great things. You've been getting me excited about my future. But I have no children! My wife is barren. We have no seed. We have no offspring."

Challenge questions:
Are you saying to God, look around, there is no way to produce any fruit and You are saying You are going to bless me, how?
Are you asking God how will You give me a seed when I'm spiritually barren?
What do you do when you have the promises of God, but you have no seed?

Seed represents evidence. If Abraham had just had one child, he could have said, "At least I have some evidence." If Sarah were pregnant, he could have said, "At least there's a child on the way." Abraham had doubt! He was on the journey to radical faith, but he wanted evidence to confirm the promise. Maybe that's where you are; needing some evidence to confirm that God will do what He has promised.

Doubt is a human response to a divine promise.

As much as we would like to believe our human response to God's promises is God said it, that settles it, therefore I believe it. Often our response is God said it, but I can't see, touch, taste, smell, or hear it, I have doubt. What am I supposed to believe? Perhaps you are struggling with addiction and God has promised you deliverance in Jesus, but you haven't seen it manifest yet. Maybe God has promised to bless you financially and yet you are still struggling. You believe God for a healthy marriage, but your marriage is still hard.

Doubt is an opportunity to draw deeper into relationship with God.

Take Your Doubt to the Right Source

Abraham could have gone to others to confirm what God said. Yet he didn't. Abraham took his doubt to the right source. When God speaks something to us, rather than us taking our doubt to the source, at times we take our doubt to other people. When you take our doubt to other people, they often make your doubt grow. Why? Because it's a human response to a divine promise. If you doubt the promises God has given you, take them to the right source. Abraham took his doubt to the right source. He talked with God.

Doubt is not an act of faithlessness it is a call to faithfulness.

Challenge questions:
Will you trust God even during your doubt?
Will you believe God even though you can't see what He's doing?
Will you believe God even though there's no evidence to support your faith in Him?

Abraham said, "God, I can't see this thing. I hear you, Lord, but I'm going to need some evidence. You're going to have to help me with this." The best part is Abraham expressed his doubt to God so He could deal with it. God's reaction was awesome. He didn't say "You big dummy. You are a faithless no-good, lousy, ungrateful servant!" Instead God said, "This man will not be your heir, but a son coming from your own body." This is huge! God said "I'm going to take Sarah's dried up womb and your old age; mix them together to produce a child. I'm going to bring life out of death." God didn't get angry. God gave him assurance. God addressed his doubt.

God will dissolve our doubt when we trust Him with it.

If you take your doubt to God, rather than Him being angry with you, He will be grateful and appreciative that you trusted Him enough to bring Him your doubts and He will dissolve it.

Do you want your doubts dissolved?

To give Abraham more assurance God said, "Wait a minute. Just in case you need some more evidence, go outside and look up. Look at the heavens and look at all the stars. Count them if you can. So shall your offspring be (Genesis 15:5, author's paraphrase)." What does that mean? God told

Abraham: "I don't care what the circumstances appear to be. I don't care what people say. It doesn't matter to me that Sarah's seventy and barren and you're eighty and dried-up. Count the stars. Just as I placed every star in the sky individually and know them by name, that's how you're going to be. I'm going to bless you to the same degree that I blessed the stars in the sky. I'm going to bless you abundantly." God not only addressed his doubt, He blew his mind.

That's God's word to you. He plans to blow your mind as you take your doubt to Him. I can see Abraham now, looking up at the sky and saying "here we go, one ...two ...three ...four ...one thousand ...oh, my, I can't count them all. It's more than I can see." That's what God is saying to you, "I will do exceedingly abundantly above all that you ask and imagine according to my riches in Christ Jesus (Ephesians 3:20)." When we trust God with our doubts, God will dissolve them.

> *"Abram believed the LORD, and he credited it to him as righteousness."*

Abraham had the nerve to believe God. He had the guts to accept the word God gave him. Many of us fail to receive from God the blessings He has for us because we fail to deal with our doubts. Many of us live beneath our privileges as children of God because we won't trust God with our doubts. Many of us have never experienced the awesome outpouring of God's anointing in our lives because we fail to deal with our doubts. Our mindset should be "I don't know how You're going to do it God. I'm not sure what, I'm not sure when, I'm not sure how. I can't see it, touch it, taste it, hear it, or smell it, but, God, you said it and that settles it. Now I'm going to wait until You do what You said You're going to do." Abraham trusted God with his doubts and God gave him assurance of the promise. Abraham believed God!

Challenge questions:
Do you believe God?
Have you taken your doubts to Him?

When doubts meet God, they dissolve.

How do our doubts dissolve when they meet God?

Here's how:

Believe God at His word

Receive assurance from God

Achieve the promise God has made you

Be like Abraham and declare, "I can't see it, smell it, taste it, touch it, or hear it. But I believe it because God said it and that settles it. Now I'm waiting. I'm working while I wait. I'm moving forward. I'm not going to stop until I get what God promised me.

The Price of Impatience

"Now Sarai, Abram's wife, had borne him no children. But she had an Egyptian maidservant named Hagar; so she said to Abram, "The LORD has kept me from having children. Go, sleep with my maidservant; perhaps I can build a family through her." Abram agreed to what Sarai said. So after Abram had been living in Canaan ten years, Sarai his wife took her Egyptian maidservant Hagar and gave her to her husband to be his wife. He slept with Hagar, and she conceived."
Genesis 16:1-4

My wife and I were expecting our first child. We were extremely excited. Everything was fine for the first fifteen weeks. At week sixteen she began having complications. By week twenty our son Josiah was born. He lived one hour twenty-three minutes. I held him in my arms as he struggled to breathe and ultimately died. Our doctor told us, had he been born one week later they could have done heroic efforts, but at twenty weeks there was nothing they could do. I learned through this experience that they make caskets in all sizes. Three years later, after a blighted ovum and losing twins to pre-term later, our daughter was born.

Through this process I learned the value of trusting God when the circumstances in your life seem hopeless.

Our Timing is not God's Timing

The account of Sarai and Hagar provides us a picture of what happens when we grow impatient while waiting on God to bring His promise to pass. Their story teaches us the price of impatience. We learn from this experience that our timing is not God's timing. Once God makes a promise, there is no way the promise will not be fulfilled. Therefore, we must trust God to fulfill the promise no matter how long it takes. Otherwise, we pay the price of impatience.

Radical faith teaches us that God's timing is not our timing!

Sarah and Abraham needed to understand this truth. Had they known this truth they would have saved themselves a lot of pain. Make sure you internalize this truth. By doing so will save you from a great deal of pain.

Ten Years is a Long Time

It has been ten years since Abraham and Sarah left Haran on faith because of God's promise. They are now in the land of Canaan. They have gone through a faith failure. They have let Lot go. They have gotten ready to get blessed. They've even received reassurance of the promise. Yet ten years is a long time to wait for anything. That is perhaps exactly what Sarah was thinking when she approached Abraham with a proposition. I can hear Sarah saying, *"We've been waiting ten years. God has told us that we're going to be parents and* there's no child to show for it. Ten years is a long time to wait."

Challenge questions:
Would you agree with Sarah that ten years is a long time to wait?
How long is too long to wait for the promise of God?

God made the promise when they were 75 and 65 respectively. Now Abraham is 85 and Sarah is 75. There still is no child. It would seem logical and even reasonable to ask the question, where is the seed?

Maybe you've been waiting on God a long time to do what He promised. You've prayed and trusted God, but He hasn't done what He promised. Maybe it's been five years or perhaps ten years; maybe even longer. You may be feeling exactly like Sarah felt. I can hear Sarah saying to Abraham, "I'm tired of waiting. I've been waiting a long time on God now. It's been ten years. God told us that He was going to give us offspring. God told us that our seed would be as numerous as the stars in the sky and the sand on the seashore. Abraham, I'm afraid that God won't do what He said He would do." You may be exactly where Sarah was. You've been believing God. You've been hoping that God would prove true. You've been waiting and waiting. You're at a point where you're beginning to wonder, is God really going to do what He promised. What makes it worse is that people can be so cruel when we are waiting on God to keep His word. They can say things that are hurtful and cause you to doubt even more. If that's where you are let me warn you: there's a price of impatience. If you take matters into your own hands, you need to know that there's a price.

You Must Know the Price of Impatience

If we are to operate in radical faith, it is crucial that we know the price of impatience.

Abraham and Sarah could have avoided the pain and problems they experienced because of their decision regarding Hagar had they known the price of impatience.

The price of impatience is determinable and destructive

You can measure the price of impatience and it produces real and dire consequences. We have evidence of these truths in the Word of God. Though it is taking a long time for God to do what He said He's going to do; though you've been waiting months, years, or even all your life; and it doesn't seem as though it's going to happen, please know there is a price of impatience.

Sarah, after waiting ten years, went to Abraham, with her own plan. She became impatient with God's plan and took matters into her own hands. Hagar was Sarah's plan. It was a destructive plan that would haunt Sarah the rest of her life.

Challenge questions:
Are you tired of waiting on God to fulfill His promise?
Do you a have plan of how you're going to get God's blessings your way?

Remember—there's a price of impatience. Hagar was a product of Abraham's faith failure. It is likely that they acquired her when they went to Egypt during the famine. She would not have even been in the house had they not had a faith failure. When we experience a faith failure, we acquire things that God did not intend for us to have. Your Hagar is a result of your faith failure. If you are not careful that which was not designed for you to have could cause you to experience pain God never intended for you to experience. From their cultural standpoint, it was okay for Sarah to give her servant to Abraham to produce a child for her. While it was culturally okay, it was not okay of God.

Everything that is culturally okay is not okay with God!

This truth is extremely relevant today. Everything that is culturally acceptable is not spiritual appropriate. God's standards supersede cultural norms and values.

This takes place after God has told Abraham, "No, Eleazar of Damascus will not inherit your wealth. But a son born of your own body will." God has told Abraham, "I'm going to bring a son through your body." God had made a promise so Abraham and Sarah should have been able to wait. Here's the truth of the matter is; you should be able to wait. God's promise doesn't have a use-by date. But Sarah grew impatient! She said, "Enough is enough. Ten years is long enough. If God was going to do it, it would have happened already. Take my servant and get me a baby. Remove the shame and the humiliation off my life." Sarah would learn the price of impatience.

By now you may be asking what qualifies me to write this book.

For nearly twenty years I have pastored a church. We have seen God do some really amazing things in the past nineteen plus years. Many people have been delivered from all kinds of addictions. We've seen people overcome many spiritual struggles. There have been people set free from years of depression and other mental illnesses. Yet the one that we have not seen is exponential growth. In a city of over 600,000 people we have not experienced significant numerical growth. There have been many times we have asked why we are not experiencing significant numerical growth. We've prayed, we've fasted, we've evangelized, there is nothing we have not tried to bring about growth. Yet, God has not chosen to bring significant growth to our church. Even as I type these words, we are still waiting on God to produce substantial growth. It would be so easy to take matters into my own hands and fabricate growth. Yet I know the price of impatience. So, we wait on God to keep His promise and do only what He can do. We refuse to pay the price of impatience.

Abraham Gives In

After Sarah presented her plan, Abraham said "Okay, let's do it." He forgot everything God said. If Abraham remembered God's promises, he would have stood up as the leader and said to Sarah, "No, God said it's through our body the seed would come." Abraham and Sarah blew it because they grew impatient. When you grow impatient, disorder occurs. When Abraham listened to Sarah the order that God created, the divine design of marriage, male and female in equal partnership with different roles and functions, was distorted. When it was distorted, the problem it produced was destructive. The consequence of the distortion was destruction. How do you know this? Keep reading to learn the answer.

It Never Works Out as Planned

After Abraham gave in and went to Hagar, two things happened: she conceived, and she began despising Sarah. The destruction started immediately. As soon as Hagar knew she was pregnant she began looking with contempt on Sarah. It didn't work out as Sarah planned. I'm sure in her mind Hagar would gladly carry her child and then give him to her once the baby was born. Yet the reality was Hagar began looking down on Sarah after she realized she was pregnant.

When you take matters in your own hands it never works out as you plan.

You can't do God's will your way. When you do the outcome will be destructive. After becoming pregnant, Hagar fell victim to pride. She began looking down on Sarah. She began looking at Sarah like, "Ha, you couldn't even have a child and you're supposed to be the mother of faith." We don't know to what degree Hagar really despised Sarah. But we do know that it led to destruction through the absence of peace. Sarah's peace was gone. I imagine she couldn't rest at night, tossing and turning on her bed. Perhaps every time she looked at Hagar, she thought, "You're carrying my blessing." When we grow impatient, our peace is stripped away. Impatience can lead to someone else carrying your blessing in their belly. Abraham and Sarah were the recipients of the promise, but Hagar was carrying it. Why? Because Sarah became impatient.

Impatience can cause your blessing to be carried in the belly of another person!

Anger Causes Irrational Actions

Sarah became angry. She grew weary of looking at Hagar. She said to Abraham, "You have to do something about this. You were supposed to lead me. You're the one who received the promise from God. You're the one God said He was going to bless and increase in number. It's your fault that I gave you Hagar." It is amazing how impatience leads to anger causing irrational actions. Sarah was irrational because of her anger. When we are impatient it often leads to anger which causes us to act irrationally.

At this point Abraham really should have stepped up to the plate and said, "Well, hold on a moment." But he didn't. He told Sarah she could do whatever she wanted to do to Hagar. Sarah began mistreating Hagar to the point that there was no peace in the house. Hagar left. The blessing walked out in her belly. Now the house was empty again. Sarah's womb was still empty. There was still no child. After taking matters into her own hands, Sarah still did not have what she was trying to get. When we become impatient with God and take matters into our own hands, we never end up getting what we are trying to get. Hagar the handmaiden ran away.

Don't let your anger cause you to act irrationally and you lose out on your blessing!

The price of impatience is first disorder, then loss of peace, and finally destruction. God declared that Ishmael would be a wild donkey of a man, his hand would be against everyone and everyone's hand would be against him. And he would live in hostility towards all his brothers (Genesis 16:12). All the trouble that continues to occur in the Middle East is because of the price of impatience. Sarah's impatient decision is still being felt today! What is the message for us? A decision you make in impatience today may affect your family for generations to come. You don't get to determine the final cost of your impatience. God told Hagar that her son Ishmael would be a wild donkey of a man who would constantly be at war. He in essence said, Ishmael will be the source of constant disorder. Every time you turn around, there will be no peace.

When you're impatient with God, the peace in your life is lost.

Finding Good News During Impatience

There is good news even amid impatience! "The angel of the Lord found Hagar near a spring in the desert. It is the spring beside the road of Shur "And he said, 'Hagar, servant of Sarai, where have you come from, and where are you going? "I'm running away from my mistress Sarai," she answered. Then the angel of the LORD told her, "Go back to your mistress and submit to her." The angel added, "I will so increase your descendants that they will be too numerous to count (Genesis 16:7-10)." God found Hagar in her distress and sent her back to Sarah. He didn't just send her back He promised to give her descendants too numerous to count. Hagar now had the same promise that Abraham and Sarah had. She became a part of God's promise because of her connection to Abraham. How did Hagar respond to God's promise? "She gave this name to the LORD who spoke to her: 'You are the God who sees me,' for she said, 'I have now seen the One who sees me (Genesis 16:13).'" Hagar came to know God for herself as the result of Sarah's impatience. She had a personal encounter with the personal God. The good news is that even in our impatience others can come to know God for themselves.

That's not the only good news. Abraham failed to lead. Sarah grew impatient. Hagar was punished by Sarah. Ishmael was born. But in the midst of this, God showed up. He met a maidservant by a spring, reached out His hand to her, lifted her up and said, "You are carrying the seed of the promise." God promised "Abraham, I will make you a great nation and I will bless those who bless you. I will curse those who curse you. And I will make your seed as numerous as the stars in the sky. And to your offspring shall I give this land." So, the God who sees, saw the seed. It may not have been in the package He intended. It may not have been in the location He intended. She was supposed to be in the house. But the God who sits high and looks low, the One who searches to and fro to find those who love Him. The God who cares for widows and orphans. Our God who cares about the hopeless, helpless and hurting looked down and saw Hagar under a tree near a spring, about to give up on life. After seeing her, God dispatched an angel to rescue her. He lifted her up and said, "I'm the God who keeps my promises. Therefore, I will bless you because you are carrying a seed of my promise."

What's the message here?

"But those who hope in the LORD will renew their strength. They will soar on wings like eagles; they will run and not grow weary, they will walk and not be faint (Isaiah 40:31)."

God's message was clear; I always keep my promise! The good news is that the one who hears and sees all will hear you in your pain, see you in your predicament and reach down from heaven to dispatch His angels to the very place where you are. He will put His arms around you and say, "I've blessed you and the seed of your loin is blessed. Everywhere you go, you will be blessed. If you will let Me, I will increase you so mightily that they won't even be able to count the increase." That's good news!

Challenge questions:
How do we find good news in the midst of our impatience?
Have you grown impatient with God?
Have you grown tired of waiting of waiting on God?
Have you become weary in your suffering?

God's Word to you today is "Wait on Me. Wherever you are in your life, I promise you if you wait, I will find you and bless you." Don't pay the price of impatience. Don't suffer the destruction that impatience produces. Yet, if you have become impatient and run from God's presence. He can find you in your place of pain and restore you to the place of promise. That's a promise!

A New Name

"When Abram was ninety-nine years old, the LORD appeared to him and said, 'I am God Almighty; walk before me and be blameless. I will confirm my covenant between me and you and will greatly increase your numbers." Abram fell facedown, and God said to him, "As for me, this is my covenant with you: You will be the father of many nations. No longer will you be called Abram; your name will be Abraham, for I have made you a father of many nations. I will make you very fruitful; I will make nations of you, and kings will come from you. I will establish my covenant as an everlasting covenant between me and you and your descendants after you for the generations to come, to be your God and the God of your descendants after you. The whole land of Canaan, where you are now an alien, I will give as an everlasting possession to you and your descendants after you; and I will be their God (Genesis 17:1-8).'"

As I have journeyed to radical faith, there have been many times when I questioned if I was truly following God's plan. As a pastor I have experienced moments when I truly wondered if I was doing the will of God. In each of those seasons God has always provided reassurance. Several years ago, now during a particularly challenging time in ministry, I was seriously *doubting if I was doing what God called me to do. I was seeking God concerning continuing Liberty and Truth Ministries. As I prayed concerning the situation, God sent the answer. I received a Facebook message from a former disciple of the ministry. She shared how her life had been completely changed by what God did through LTM. She shared how she had grown so much and was continuing to grow because of the teaching she received. I knew this was God answering my prayer and reassuring me I was doing His will.*

Maybe you are wondering if you are doing God's will. Please know if you seek Him, he will give you the answer you need to reassure you. That's what He did for Abraham. That's what He did for me. He will do the same for you.

The Promise is Worth the Wait

Ishmael was born. He represented the price of impatience. Abraham was now ninety-nine years old. It has been twenty-four since God made the promise to him. Yet, at ninety-nine, Abraham is still before God in obedience waiting for the fulfillment. Ponder that—twenty-four long years. It had to appear as though it wasn't going to happen. It's nearly a quarter of a century later. Can't you hear Abraham, "We've blown it. Our faith failure must have disqualified us from the promise. We let Lot go; but maybe we waited too long to do so. We've been getting ready to get blessed for so long, I don't even remember what is going on. Sarah is now eighty-nine and I'm ninety-nine. I've waited, faithfully. I left everything I knew and traveled to this place. I'm living here as an alien. Now what? Surely God must have forgotten. He said He was going to do it, and now look! Ishmael is 13 years old. He's getting to the age of accountability, and maybe God changed his mind." Abraham was probably struggling significantly as he watched Ishmael grow up and still did not have a child by Sarah.

You may have been waiting so long for God to do what He said He was going to do in your life, that you're thinking it will never happen. You have been going through in obedience; fasting, praying, giving faithfully, and serving sacrificially. You have been living to please the Lord. Yes, you've had a few faith failures. Yes, there were some Lots in your life, but you let them go. Yes, you've been getting ready to get blessed. You want to believe God, yet in the back your mind, every time you look at your Ishmael (that thing in your life that is there because of your impatience), you think it's too late.

Ishmael is the visible representation of your impulsivity.

He reminds you every time you look at him that your impatience produced this. Perhaps you are thinking; surely, now I won't get blessed. After all, you can only blow it so many times. You say to yourself; I know He's the God of second chances, but at some point He stops giving chances. You begin to think, "This isn't going to happen. Is it? Because, if it was, I wouldn't still be waiting." If that's where you are, let me encourage you with these words—the promise is worth the wait. You have come too far to give up now. God has not forgotten you and all His promises are yes in Christ Jesus. Now declare your Amen in agreement with God's promise.

I know what I'm talking about because I've seen God keep His promise. When we moved into our ministry headquarters in 2004. God had me begin praying for Him to release the buildings on the entire block into our heads. We prayed and waited from 2004 to 2010 for the manifestation of the promise. Then one afternoon the president and vice president of the bank that owned the property directly adjacent to our building walked in and said they were looking for an organization in the neighborhood that might be interested in acquiring the property. For several months we discussed and negotiated with them regarding purchasing the property. Then on December 24, 2010 I received an email from the Vice President stating the board of the bank had met and decided the best way to support our mission was the donate the property to us. God kept His word. Once we received the donation, we had to raise the money to renovate the building for occupancy. It took another four years to raise the money, but in October 2014 we had raised all the money needed to complete all the renovations. We now have not one ministry headquarters, but three facilities through which to serve the community. God always keeps His word! I could go on to share how we had to raise several thousand dollars in thirty days to keep the city from foreclosing on the property because the previous owner had several years' worth of unpaid water bills and how God released the funds for us to pay it off just in the nick of time.

I know God never changes His mind when He makes a promise. Just as God didn't change His mind for us, I'm convinced of the same for you.

Radical faith knows that God never changes His mind when He makes a promise

Challenge question:
How does one remain faithful when there is no proof of the promise?

Remaining Faithful When There's No Proof of the Promise

You may be wondering that as you wait on God to do what He promised. Maybe you're even raising the question, "Has God changed His mind?" You need to know He hasn't changed His mind. He hasn't recanted His promise. God wants you to know that He is giving you a new name as proof of His commitment to keep His promise. I can hear God in the spirit realm saying, "I know that you're beginning to doubt Me. I know it's beginning to feel as though it's just not going to happen. Your friends are starting to laugh. Your family is starting to doubt if what you say God has promised you will ever manifest. After all there is no tangible evidence that God is doing what you said He promised to do." This may be hard to believe but, God wants you to know, He's changing your name. He's giving you a new name.

Why a new name? Because historically a person's name represented the content of their character. Proverbs 22:1 says "a good name is to be chosen rather than great riches." One's name defines who one is. So, God is saying to you today, "I'm giving you a new name, because the name that you have now doesn't capture the content of your character. The name that you have now, doesn't represent the richness of your heritage. The name that you now have, doesn't define the wholeness that I'm bringing about in you. So, I'm giving you a new name."

Challenge questions:
Are you ready to receive a new name?
Are you ready to receive the name God has for you?

I hope that you are because the new name God is giving you is proof of His commitment to keep His promise. Maybe you are struggling to receive what is being said. Let me provide scriptural support for it. 2 Corinthians 5:17 declares, "If anyone is in Christ he is a new creation, behold the old has gone and the new has come (author paraphrase)." In Ephesians 4:22-24 we are told the believers have put off their old self and put on the new self which is in the likeness of God. In fact, throughout the New Testament we are instructed that in Christ we become new! We are given a new name when we come to faith in Christ. We are no longer sinners, we are saints of God (see, Romans 12:13, Ephesians 3:18, Philippians 4:22, and 2 Corinthians 13:13).

Abram (the name he was given by his father) is now 99. Sarai (the name she was given by her father) is 89. Haran is a distant memory. Lot's living in Sodom. Ishmael has reached puberty. God showed up on the scene again saying the same thing. Think about it, 24 years have passed. Yet God shows up saying the same thing "Hey, Abram, I'm ready. I'm going to bless you and I'm going to make you a great nation. I'm going to increase you in number. I'm going to make you a prosperous tree." It's the same thing again. That may be where you are right now. You know all the promises God has given you, yet you are still going through the same thing. You may be saying to yourself, "God, I'm tired of hearing it." I can imagine Abraham said, "God, don't you know? We've been down this road before. I've listened to You now for 24 years and all I have to show for it is an Ishmael. I don't have anything else to show for it. All I have to show is an Ishmael." Let me encourage you, don't give up and decide there is no hope because "God is not a man that He should lie, nor the son of man that He should change His mind (Numbers 23:19)."

It's the Same Message, but Different Actions

God was speaking the same message to Abram, but He did some things differently. He was about to change Abram's name.

What did God do differently?

He identified Himself differently

God said, "I am God Almighty." The Hebrew is "El Shaddai." What was He really saying? God was saying, "I'm God who is enough. I'm God all-sufficient. I'm God who doesn't need any help from anybody else to do what I'm going to do. I'm God who can stand on my own against every force in the universe and be victorious. I'm God Almighty." Receive that truth today. God is sufficient in Himself to do what He has promised.

Abram needed to hear that because just a few years ago, he tried to take matters into his own hand to produce the seed of the promise his own way. Likewise, you need to know He's God Almighty. He does not need your help to do what He said He's going to do in your life. All He needs you to do is get in line with His will. Because if you're lined up with His will, He'll bring it to pass. He's God Almighty. God is God all by Himself. He has all power and He doesn't need us to help. He just needs us to line up.

He called Abraham to sincere obedience

God said, "I am God Almighty; walk before me and be blameless." He really was saying to Abram and to us, "I'm about to give you a new name, but the first thing you have to do is be sincerely obedient." This word is interesting, "Walk before Me and be blameless." We think that means to be perfect. But God is really saying to Abram, "Walk before Me in sincerity. Walk before Me in integrity." Another way of saying that is, "Just be real with me." Often, we think God wants us to be perfect. Yet, that's not the case.

God isn't concerned with our perfection He's concerned with our realness

He wants us to be real before Him. God says to Abram, "Walk before Me in the wholeness of who you are. Walk before Me in realness." If we're going to have a new name, we must walk before God in realness. We must take the mask off and be real with God. We must get to the point in our lives where we say, "God, I'm tired of faking. I'm tired of pretending. I'm tired of fronting. I just want to be real." God, this time, tells Abram, "If you're going to get the promise, you've got to be real." God's word to us is you've got to be real. If we are to experience all God has for us, we must operate in integrity. Being real is congruence between our public and private self. It's being the same in all environments.

Challenge questions:
Are you ready to be real with God?
What masks are you wearing that need to come off?

It is important to realize that the promise that God has for us cannot be received until we pay the cost. The cost attached to the promise is realness. It's time to be real with God in order to receive the promise He has for you!

There's Only One Proper Response

When God began speaking to Abram, he fell down before Him. Abram didn't know anything else to do but fall down in humble worship. We often miss what God has to say because when He begins to speak, we are too full of ourselves to be humble and listen. Proverbs 16:18 states, "Pride goes before destruction and a haughty spirit before a fall." Pride keeps us from receiving the promise of God. As God began speaking, Abram fell facedown. Then God said, "I'm going to give you a new name." "Abram" meant "exalted father." "Abraham" means "father of many." There's not much of a difference there. "Exalted father" and "father of many." But one represents his past and his present, "exalted father," with one son, Ishmael. A son not even of the covenant because God later tells him, "No, Ishmael is not the child of the promise. No, I didn't make My covenant with Ishmael." Abraham represented his future. God intended to bless every nation of the world through Abraham. His new name represented his promised future.

Today God is looking for believers who are humble enough to bow in His presence. He is searching men and women who recognize Him for who He is and humble themselves before Him. These humble saints of God will position themselves to have God change their names. They will receive a name from God that fits with their promised future. In Revelation 3:12 we read these words, "He who overcomes, I will make him a pillar in the temple of My God, and he will not go out from it anymore, and I will write on him the name of My God, and the name of the city of My God, the new Jerusalem, which comes down out of heaven from My God, and My new name." That is God's promise to the church at Philadelphia found in Revelation and by extension I am convinced it's His promise to us.

Challenge question:
Will you humble yourself so that God can put His name on you and give you what He has promised you?

If you will look forward to receiving all that God has promised those who are the seed of Abraham, why do I say that?

Because God went on to tell Abraham He would do three things for him:

1. I will make you fruitful
2. I will make an everlasting covenant with you and your offspring
3. I will give you all the land of Canaan

Everything God promised Abraham as the father of faith, is ours by faith. Now that's good news! Receive the new name God has for you. Recognize God for who He is, serve Him in realness, and humble yourself in worship before Him. He has given you a new name!

Redeeming the Remnant

"When the men got up to leave, they looked down toward Sodom, and Abraham walked along with them to see them on their way. Then the LORD said, 'Shall I hide from Abraham,'" it's like God's having a thought to Himself, "'what I am about to do? Abraham will surely become a great and powerful nation, and all nations on earth will be blessed through him. For I have chosen him, so that he will direct his children and his household after him to keep the way of the LORD by doing what is right and just, so that the LORD will bring about for Abraham what he has promised him.' Then the LORD said, 'The outcry against Sodom and Gomorrah is so great and their sin so grievous that I will go down and see if what they have done is as bad as the outcry that has reached me. If not, I will know.' The men turned away and went toward Sodom, but Abraham remained standing before the LORD. Then Abraham approached him and said: 'Will you sweep away the righteous with the wicked? What if there are fifty righteous people in the city? Will you really sweep it away and not spare the place for the sake of the fifty righteous people in it? Far be it from you to do such a thing-to kill the righteous with the wicked, treating the righteous and the wicked alike. Far be it from you! Will not the Judge of all the earth do right? (Genesis 18:16-25)'"

Radical Faith Calls Us to Intercede for Others

September 11, 2001 was a day I will never forget. I was at work when the planes hit the World Trade Center towers. I remember gathering with my staff around a television watching in horror as the second plane hit. We were speechless. Three months later we were still dealing with the aftermath of the greatest act of terror on U.S. soil in history. It was then that I stood to minister the words that are found in this chapter. I entitled the sermon Redeeming the Remnant: The Power of Intercessory Prayer.

Hear now the first few words of the sermon I preached that day: "We live in a time of great wickedness. All types of inhumane and indecent acts are being perpetrated against men, women, and children. Many are still dealing with the catastrophic events that are dealing with September 11th. Some lost friends, some lost family members, some lost fortunes. Some lost all kinds of things at the hands of terrorists. Others are dealing with their own pain of being mentally, physically, emotionally, sexually, and many times spiritually abused. There is great wickedness in the land. Children are being exploited... There is great wickedness in the land. Am I telling the truth? Yet, when I really think about this situation, when I look at all the wickedness, I hear a small, quiet voice, when I listen, crying out to be saved. I hear this small, quiet voice that's crying out to be saved. There is a righteous remnant who live among the wicked and perhaps are even at times caught up in the wickedness. But they cry out, "Lord, save us." There are those who are not content even though they're living in a land filled with wickedness, they're not content to live in the wickedness and they really want to be redeemed."

It takes radical faith to intercede for those who are caught up in the wickedness of the sinful world and want to get out, but do not know how. We are called to redeem the remnant. This is done through intercessory prayer. Upon learning about God's plan to destroy Sodom and Gomorrah, Abraham interceded with God on behalf of Lot. This teaches us the power of intercessory prayer.

There is a Remnant

Here's a stark reality: we live in a world filled with wickedness. We are living in neighborhoods and communities filled with wickedness. In fact, we were all once a part of the wickedness of the world. Yet God prompted someone to pray for our redemption. I submit that every person who has ever been saved, was brought to salvation by the prayers of the righteous remnant.

In every community, no matter how wicked, there is a righteous remnant.

It may not be large, but there is a remnant who are living for God. The remnant may be caught up among the wicked, but they want to be redeemed and live for God. There's a remnant in every community. You may say, "Well, not where I live, they're all wicked. Not where I work, they're all wicked. Not in my school, they're all wicked." It may seem that way but, there is a remnant! In the most wicked society, there's a remnant that wants to be redeemed, that's crying out to be healed, and that longs for salvation.

It seems that Abraham knew this and when given the opportunity, he interceded before God Almighty on their behalf. As Abraham was on his journey towards radical faith, he redeemed the remnant through the power of intercessory prayer. Let us discover how to redeem the remnant through the power of intercessory prayer.

Definitions are Important

I've discovered that definitions are important. I am convinced that until we know the meaning of something, we cannot understand it. Therefore, let's begin with some definitions. We will need these to continue our journey to radical faith.

"To redeem" means to "claim back, to salvage, to restore, to make good again."

A "remnant" is "a small group among a larger number."

We're talking about claiming back, salvaging, restoring, reclaiming and making good again a small group among a larger number. In every wicked nation, state, city, or neighborhood, there is a small group of people who are not content with the wickedness. There is a group of discontent people caught up in the wickedness around them who are ready to be redeemed. I do not know the size of the group in your particular context, but I know there is a remnant, that says, "We want out. If anybody would come and teach us and show us the way, we'd leave."

Knowing that a remnant is a small group among a larger group is important because it helps us narrow our focus as we intercede for their redemption. We pray for the salvation of all the lost, but we focus on redeeming the remnant who are ready to be saved.

Intimacy Produces Inclusion

The responsibility of those who have radical faith is to find the remnant and engage in intercessory prayer so that God uses us to redeem them. It's our responsibility.

How is it done?

It begins in conversation with God. Abraham and God were in conversation. As they walk, God starts thinking and then says, "Should I tell Abraham what I'm about to do. I'm about to take these cities out. Should I tell him?" He then reasons to Himself and says, "I don't have a choice because we're too close. There's too much intimacy between Abraham and I, I have to let him know my plans." This lets us know that intimacy produces inclusion.

When we are intimate with God, He includes us in His plans. The closer one becomes with God, the more God tells them His plans. If you're wondering why it never seems like you hear the voice of God, perhaps it's because you and God are not close enough yet. Perhaps it's because there is not enough intimacy. When you get close to God, He will begin to tell you His plans.

There are times when God arrests my attention and tells me something that is going on in this person's life or that person's family. He may give me a word of warning for a person concerning something in which they are involved. Usually when this happens, I always find myself praying for the person.

You should want to be so intimate with God that He says I must tell her/him what I'm about to do. As God walks with Abraham and the angels He says, "Should I tell Abraham? What a foolish thought, how could I not tell him?" God says, "For I have known him, in order that he may command his children and his household after him, that they keep the way of the LORD, to do righteousness and justice, that the LORD may bring to Abraham what He has spoken to him (Genesis 18:19 NKJV)." That speaks directly to intimacy and inclusion. Look at these words, "For I have known him." He knew Him—that implies they had a close relationship. God and Abraham were close. When we get close with God, He begins to include us in His plans. Intimacy produced inclusion. The closer we become with God, the more He shares His plans with us. God knew Abraham and Abraham knew God.

Challenge questions
How intimately do you feel with God?
Does He tell you His plans?
Are you ready for that level of intimacy?

Intimacy is Developed through Worship

How do we develop the level of intimacy that Abraham had with God? That level of intimacy is produced through worship. Throughout Abraham's journey to radical faith, he worshipped God. In Genesis 12:7-9, Abraham is between Bethel and Ai and it says, "Then Abraham called on the name of the Lord." That's worship. Genesis 13:4 says, "Abraham called on the Name of the Lord." That's worship. Genesis 13:18, says Abraham built an altar to the Lord. That's worship. In Chapter 15 God and Abraham are in this intimate relationship of worship throughout the chapter. Throughout Abraham's journey to radical faith, he worshipped God. If you want intimacy with God, you must be a worshipper.

Going to church does not equal worship. Worship is a lifestyle of giving God the adoration and honor He deserves. A worshipper is someone who gets into the presence of God, forgets about everything else, and pours out their spirit to God. Abraham called on the Name of the Lord. He was a worshipper. If you want to be included in God's plans, you must learn to call on His Name. Calling on His name involves putting everything else out of your mind and being present with the Lord. In a world that is always focused on what's next on the to-do list, worship calls for us to press pause and bow in God's presence. Abraham knew how to worship; as a result, he and God became intimate. God inhabits the praises of His people Israel (Psalm 22:3). It is worship that produces the intimacy with God that causes Him to include you in His plans.

Spiritual Principle: Worship develops intimacy with God

The Challenge of Knowing God's Plans

Abraham and God were so tight that God said, "I'm have to tell him." God tells Abraham, *"I need to let you know something. There's an outcry going on. I know your nephew's down in Sodom. But there's something that's been ringing in my ears. There's a buzzing, a ringing, a cry, and it's in my ears."* That's what God said to Abraham. *"It's the cry of wickedness coming up from the cities on the plain. I want you to know because I trust you with my plans. I want you to know I'm on my way down there. I'm going there to check it out. I'm going* to look and see. Abraham, if I look and it's as bad as I think it is, I'm wiping them out. They can't live in wickedness any longer. I'm sick of it (author's paraphrase)." God included Abraham.

Why did God include Abraham?

I'm convinced He didn't tell Abraham so Abraham would say, "You're right, God. Those folks down there sure are bad. I told Lot not to go down there. I told him, I said, 'if you go there, it's going to be a mess.'" God told Abraham His plans because He knew Abraham would do something with the information. When God includes us in His plans, He is counting on us to do something with the information. That is the challenge of knowing God's plans. He wants us to respond in a way that moves Him to action.

God tells us His plans so that we will do something with the information

Why does God want us to do something with the information?

Because wickedness produces an outcry in the presence of God. We read, "Then the LORD said, 'The outcry against Sodom and Gomorrah is so great and their sin so grievous that I will go down and see if what they have done is as bad as the outcry that has reached me (Genesis 19:20 and 21).'" This is an important principle for us to know: God knows about the wickedness that is happening in the world. He hears and sees all that is happening. Don't think that God doesn't know about the wickedness. God knows, God sees, and God hears the wickedness. He listens, He observes, He waits, and when it finally reaches a certain level, God says,

"That's it. I'm going to go down and I'm going to deal with it myself." Please know that God sees and knows exactly what is happening. He will give time for repentance, but then God will act! Wickedness will not prevail in the end.

God tells Abraham His plans and he instantly acts! I can hear Abraham now, *"Hold on, wait a minute, God. You mean to tell me that You're going to go down there and you're going to wipe out all the righteous people with the wicked?"* Abraham was moved to act. When you have been included in the plans of God, inclusion produces intercession. God doesn't include us in His plans to do nothing. God includes us so that we will begin interceding. Once Abraham received the information from God, He stood in the gap for the righteous remnant saying, *"God, I believe that there's at least some people down in Sodom who are not wicked."* You must believe that no matter what the situation is, there are some people who are not wicked. You must believe that no matter how bad it looks, there's a remnant. After all, Lot and his family made up four righteous people. Abraham assumed that Lot would be righteous. Four equals a remnant. So, he began praying.

Four Characteristics of Intercession

I want to end this chapter by giving four characteristics of intercession: urgency, sincerity, boldness, and persistence.

A Sense of Urgency
In order to be an intercessor, there must be a sense of urgency. You must feel like it's got to happen, that you must do something right now. Urgency presses you into action. You sense that there is no time to waste. It is clear that Abraham had urgency. He felt pressed to act. He

immediately began interceding to God on behalf of the righteous remnant in Sodom and Gomorrah.

Sincerity
Sincerity is genuineness in attitude and action. It is doing the right thing for the right reason. Abraham acted in sincerity. He was genuinely concerned for the righteous remnant and he was equally concerned about God preserving His character. Sincerity moved Abraham to intercede. Intercession must be done with sincerity.

Boldness
There must be a spirit of boldness also. You must be bold before God on behalf of the righteous remnant. Boldness causes you to take risks in prayer. It causes you to push the envelope with God. Abraham was bold in his intercession. He pushed the envelope. He was not concerned about protecting himself, he was concerned about redeeming the remnant.

Persistence
Finally, there must be persistence. You must remain in God's presence until He does what you want Him to do. Persistence is staying the course. It is continuing until something changes. Abraham persisted in prayer until God agreed to redeem the righteous. He kept praying until God heard him and responded in the way he wanted to hear.

Abraham interceded saying, "Will you sweep away the righteous with the wicked?" He had a sense of urgency. He didn't waste time. As soon as God said it, he started moving, he started communicating with God. That's how it is. As soon as God reveals His plans to us regarding what He's doing in the earth realm, we should instantly start praying.

We should instantly fall on our face before God. Why? Because there is no time to waste. In the midst of wickedness, we are to be interceding on behalf of the righteous remnant who are caught up with the wicked. We should intercede that God would release them and bring them to repentance. Abraham acted immediately. He asked the question, "God, isn't there a difference? I know that it's great wickedness, but isn't there a difference? Are you going to treat the righteous just like the wicked?" He began to pray. He said, *"What if there are fifty righteous people there. God, hold on. What if there are fifty? I mean, come on God, there's at least fifty. Okay, God, well maybe there's not fifty. Let's say there's five less, only forty-five."* He's persisting now. He's bold. And God says, *"Okay, if there's forty-five."* Then Abraham says, *"Well, God, I don't mean any harm. Maybe there aren't forty-five, there may only be forty."* He said, *"Okay, for forty."* "Okay, God, maybe there aren't quite forty righteous there. Maybe there's only thirty. You mean You're going to destroy a whole city when there are thirty righteous people?" God said, "No, I won't destroy them." "God, I mean, now that I've been so bold in Your presence, I have the spirit of boldness now. But, God, what if there are only twenty?" "For twenty I won't." And he said, "Well, God, since I've been this crazy, since I've pushed You to the limit. Since You are so powerful, since You are so just, since You are so righteous and so merciful, what if there are only ten?" Then God says, "For the sake of ten, I won't destroy the city." After that Abraham stopped, he knew he had gone as far with God as he could. When you are an intercessor and you have an intimate relationship with God, you will know how far to go with God. When you go as far as you can go, stop. That's it. Abraham stopped. It's important to learn when to stop. Yes, we need to be bold enough to push God as far as we can, but we also need to know when to stop.

Intimacy Teaches Us to be Bold and Persistent

Remember Abraham knew God and God knew Abraham. Many Christians can't be bold and persistent in God's presence because there is not enough intimacy in our relationship with Him.

What prevents us from being bold and persistent in God's presence?

When we don't spend enough time with God on a regular basis to know His heart, we can't be bold and persistent in His presence. The more intimate we are with God, the more we can push the limits of His righteousness and patience.

Here's an example from my life. *My wife knows me very well. Therefore, she can say things to me that other people can't say to me. She can ask things of me that others can't ask of me. Very early on it became apparent that God had shown her enough of my heart that she knew how to talk to me.* I would tell her, "You know, I really appreciate it that you know how to talk to me." That's based on intimacy. O, that we would get that way with God so that we know how to talk with Him. You should be so intimate with God that you can say, "Listen, God, You told me in Your Word that You would not allow anything to come on me that You couldn't handle on my behalf. You told me in Your Word that by Your stripes I am healed. You told me in Your Word that I am more than a conqueror. Therefore, God, I'm expecting to be victorious." That's intimacy.

Intimacy produces inclusion
   Inclusion produces intercession
      Intercession produces divine intervention

God Wants to See for Himself

After Abraham prayed, God and the angels went down to Sodom. In Sodom it was just as bad as they thought it was. When the angels arrived there, the men of the city were so perverted that they wanted to rape them. These were male angels. It was heinous to God that these people would have no more regard for strangers than to want to take them and abuse them. Therefore, the decision was made to destroy the wicked cities Sodom and Gomorrah. God didn't decide to destroy these cities without first seeing for Himself if the people were as wicked as He was told. Once He saw for Himself, God knew the cities must be destroyed.

In Psalm 37:1 and 2 we read "Do not fret because of evildoers, be not be envious toward wrongdoers. For they will wither quickly like the grass and fade like the green herb." God will act to judge the wicked!

But what about Lot, his wife, and his two daughters. Remember, Abraham interceded. When the angels arrived, Lot takes them in. He says, "I'll protect you." He takes them into his home and the men of the city want to kill Lot. If the angels had not snatched Lot back into the house, he would have been killed. Even still the men of the city were determined to abuse the strangers. Wickedness knows no boundaries! The angels said to Lot, "You and your family and anybody else that's with you, you all need to leave here because we're about to destroy this city." Lot went out to his sons-in-law to convince them to leave with his family, but they refused. It was then that it became clear that there were not even ten righteous people in the city. What would God do now that there were not even ten righteous people in the city? He would keep His word. That is good news for

That meant God was committed to redeeming Lot and his family.

Let that encourage you to intercede for the righteous remnant. God is committed to keeping His word. He will always redeem the righteous remnant.

Radical faith moves us to intercede for the righteous remnant

Your Intercession Brings about the Redemption of Others

When it became clear the cities of Sodom and Gomorrah would be destroyed, Lot begged the angel, "Let me go over here to this little city?" The angel said, "Very well, go. I'll grant this request also." I imagine Lot must have thought, "What do you mean you will grant that request also?" Lot didn't know that Abraham, by the trees of Mamre, had interceded to God on his behalf. Before the angels ever arrived at the city of Sodom, he had already had a request granted that any righteous people there would be spared. So, when Lot said, "Can I go over here," the angel said, "Very well, go. I'm going to grant you this request also." When we intercede on the behalf of others, our intercession brings about their deliverance without them even knowing we have interceded. Let this sink in, when we intercede for the remnant, God will reach down and redeem them out of the wickedness and they don't even have to know you were praying. By interceding for others, we may pray forth household salvation. Our family may get saved, our loved ones may get saved, even out coworkers may get saved because we intercede on their behalf. The best part of it is they don't even have to know that we were the ones praying for them. That's the power of intercessory prayer.

One final thought. "So when God destroyed the cities of the plain, He remembered Abraham, and He brought Lot out of the catastrophe that overthrew the cities where Lot had lived (Genesis 19:29)." When we grasp the power of intercessory prayer, we will begin to cry out to God so that He will reach down among the wicked and redeem the righteous remnant. There are people in your family, in your community, and on your job that are caught up in wickedness right now and it doesn't look good. But you must understand that when the saints of God begin to intercede on their behalf it will move God to action and the remnant that is righteous will be redeemed.

Here's a word of encouragement; instead of giving up on those who seem to be caught up in wickedness, intercede for them. When you intercede it moves God to intervene. There is always a remnant in the midst of the wicked who want to be redeemed. God has given us the power to bring about their redemption. What is our power? Our power is intercessory prayer. I encourage you to use the power of intercessory prayer to move God to redeem the righteous remnant.

Move in radical faith to redeem the remnant through intercessory prayer

And Sarah Laughed

"Where is your wife Sarah?' they asked him. 'There, in the tent,' he said. Then the LORD said, 'I will surely return to you about this time next year, and Sarah your wife will have a son.' Now Sarah was listening at the entrance to the tent, which was behind him. Abraham and Sarah were already old and well advanced in years, and Sarah was past the age of childbearing. So Sarah laughed to herself as she thought, 'After I am worn out and my master is old, will I now have this pleasure? (Genesis 18:9-12)'"

A Testimony Worth Hearing

The date was Sunday, November 11, 2001. I stood to minister the word of God to the saints at Liberty and Truth Ministries. As I stood to minister, I heard myself saying these words, "I'm at a place in my life where I don't know anything else to do but trust God. I mean, let me just get real for a minute. I've tried everything else. I've tried drugs, they didn't work. I've tried crime, and even during the tears, the pain was still there. I've tried drinking. Nope, it doesn't make the pain go away. I tried sleeping around, and it didn't work either. Nothing has worked except God in my life. And during my pain, I have reached the place where all I know to do is trust God. I thought if I was popular, if people liked me, if folks thought I was cool, then that would make me feel good. All that did was make me feel good when they were there. But the instant they left, I was still in the same shape. You know, I'm at a point now where all I know to do is trust God. I tried living life without Him. I tried doing it on my own. I tried doing it the way I thought it ought to be done. I tried all of that."

Why am I retelling this account from so many years ago and what does it have to do with radical faith?

I want you to know that this is a testimony worth hearing. As you read the words of this testimony and this book, you may be thinking to yourself, "I'm going to keep trying. I'm going to keep doing what I want to do." I want to let you know that I've discovered that it doesn't work. You may need to go through it for yourself, but sometimes you should not have to experience things for yourself to believe. You should be able to take the word of somebody else. I know experience is a good teacher. Yet, sometimes it's an unnecessary teacher. Sometimes you should be able to receive a word from someone else and save yourself some pain. None of the things in the world can heal the hurt and pain you have experienced; only God can. So, with this in mind let's drop in on Abraham and Sarah again.

Serving Opens Doors

God and Abraham were in conversation. Sarah stood at the door of the tent. God shared with Abraham that He was about to finally fulfill the promise. It was so surprising that we find these words recorded "So Sarah laughed to herself..." The question is why did she laugh?

Here's the backdrop. After twenty-four years, God showed up at their house to pay them a visit. He didn't come alone this time. He brought with Him two strangers that many believe to be angels. When Abraham saw them, he instantly went into servant mode. He said, "Come over and sit down." He began preparing them a meal, while bringing something to drink. Abraham went all out; he even killed the fattened calf. He served the meal and stood guard in the posture of a servant waiting just in case they needed something. As Abraham was serving them, God began to talk to him. God said, "Where is your wife, Sarah?" Not, "Where's Hagar?" Hagar was the mistress, but Sarah was the wife. He said, "Where is the one I've given you? Where is the one I promised to bring your seed through?" Abraham responded, Lord, she's over there in the tent. She's over there doing what she's supposed to do when men are doing what they are supposed to do." As Abraham served God, God began to speak to him about fulfilling the promise. The point is: serving opens the door for God to move in your life. If you are to operate in radical faith to receive the promise of God, you must be willing to serve the Lord while you wait.

Serving moves God to action!

The Importance of Knowing How God Operates

Until now God had not dealt with Sarah. He had not spoken to Sarah at all. Every promise He made had been to Abraham. Sarah, being the helpmeet, being one who understood divine order, was going along just because Abraham believed God. There's something to be said about divine order. Please to do not misunderstand what I am about to say. I am not in any way minimizing or criticizing single women. But in marriage, God gives the man a vision. The man then must share the vision with his wife. When he shares the vision with his wife, if she understands divine order, she'll get in line with the vision. When he gets in line and she gets in line, then the vision can go forth. It's important to know how God operates. If you are single, God gives you the vision directly. Yet, if you are married, there is an order to how God operates when giving vision.

God was now ready to speak to Sarah. "Where's Sarah? I want to talk to her this time. I need to get a message through to her." If you are a Sarah type, I want you to know God wants to talk to you. He wants to get a word through to you. He is saying, "Where is Sarah?" Abraham says, "She's there in the tent." What happens next is really powerful. It's as if God knew Sarah was listening and said (I'm paraphrasing), *"This time next year, I'm going to come back. And when I come back, what's been empty is going to be full. When I come back, the place where you've been hurting will be healed. When I come back, your barrenness will be blessed and you'll have a child."* Just as God was trying to get Sarah's attention, He is trying to get your attention to let you know that He's closer to fulfilling what He's promised than it seems. Though for a little while it may seem that He is distant. He's not distant, He's working in you to get you to the place to receive the promise. God is working behind the scene and when He reappears, it will be time for the manifestation of the promise. God said to Abraham, "at this time next year I will return and your wife Sarah will have a son." That's how God operates. He moves according to His timetable not ours.

Spiritual Principle: If we are to live in radical faith, we must understand how God operates.

It's Not as Long as It Seems

I'm sure a year seems like a long time when you're ninety-nine years old and you've been waiting twenty-four years for the promise to be fulfilled. I can hear Abraham thinking to himself "A year from now. You want me to wait another whole year? I've been waiting all this time and you mean to tell me it's going to be a whole year before I receive what You promised twenty-four years ago?" Sarah was standing in the door of the tent and she heard what God said. I imagine she began thinking, "I'm eighty-nine years old. Abraham is ninety-nine years old. How in the world is this going to happen?" Abraham and Sarah were already old and well advanced in years. Sarah was past the age of childbearing. Humanly, this wasn't possible. From a human perspective, this was a medical impossibility. If it was already impossible from a human perspective, another year would only make it that much more impossible. A year is a long time from a human perspective, but it's not long when you are operating in divine time. In 2 Peter 3:8 we read, "But do not let this one fact escape your notice, beloved, that with the Lord one day is like a thousand years, and a thousand years is like one day."

Radical faith tells us it's not as long as it seems!

Often God doesn't even intervene until all the human options have already been exhausted. Many times, He doesn't even show up until you've done everything you know how to do. It's only when you have exhausted your options, that Go then moves. When your options have been exhausted, you are primed and ready to receive the promise of God. I have discovered that as long as we're still working things out, we are not ready to receive what God has promised. It's when we finally stop striving that God shows up and acts. Somebody is raising the question "Why is that?" Because if the human options are open, we may take the credit ourselves instead of giving it to God. Some people can't receive the blessings and promises that God has for them because when He blesses, they think they did it. We must be careful that when God gives us what He promised, instead of giving Him the glory, we take the glory for ourselves.

It's Ridiculous, But Real

"This time next year, I'm going to show up and I'm going to give you what I promised you." That's what God said to Abraham. When Sarah heard this, she laughed. She laughed. Why did she laugh? Try to put yourself in Sarah's shoes. You've been waiting twenty-four years, you're almost ninety years old, your husband is almost a hundred years old and God shows up at your doorstep saying, "This time next year I'm going to show up and you're going to have a son." I can hear myself thinking, "How ridiculous! Why is God picking on me?" I can hear Sarah laughing to herself, thinking, "Why in the world would God mess with me like this? Why is He playing with me? Is He trying to make me the laughingstock of the community? Why is God telling me this when every option has already been exhausted?" There are times when God says things to us that don't seem realistic. In those times we need radical faith to realize, it's ridiculous, but it's real!

Challenge questions:
Has God ever told you something that seemed impossible? What do you do when what God is promising is so ridiculous that it doesn't make sense?

Sarah laughed! You may be laughing right now when you think about God's promises. God has promised to move in your life in ways that seem ridiculous and you're thinking to yourself, "There's no way." The word of God is filled with promises that seem to be ridiculous, yet they are real. We know that because we read *"For as many as are the promises of God, in Him they are yes; therefore, also through Him is our Amen to the glory of God through us (2 Corinthians 1:20)."* You may be like Sarah and laugh at God's promises. She laughed and said, *"Now God is really picking on me. He's talking to me about having a baby when I'm about to be ninety years old. He's talking to me about having a baby when I know that it will never happen."* It's ridiculous, but it's real. God can do what seems impossible. God's word declares, "Is there anything too hard for God?"

Radical faith knows God's promises are ridiculous but real!

Challenge questions:
Do you have the faith to believe God's promises although they are ridiculous? Will you push past your doubt and trust God's word?

There's an Answer for Your Laughter

You may be in a place where you feel like you've been set up for disappointment. You've tried everything you know to try and instead of getting better, things have become worse. That's perhaps how Sarah felt. She laughed. Even though right now you may be laughing and thinking, "It is not going to happen. God isn't going to answer my prayers." Please know God has an answer for your laughter.

Challenge question:
How do you hold on to faith when it seems like God has set you up for disappointment?

Don't think that because the promise seems like an impossibility God doesn't have an answer. "Then the LORD said to Abraham, 'Why did Sarah laugh and say, 'Will I really have a child, now that I am old?' Is anything too hard for the LORD?'"

The Lord's response to our laughter is to raise the question,

"Why are you laughing?"

We're not used to God asking us questions. We're used to God telling us things. But He raised the question, "Why is Sarah laughing?" That's the question God wants to know today. "Why are you laughing?" Laughter is often an indication of doubt. When we question if God will do what He said He will do, we laugh. Laughter is also an indication of fear. When we are too afraid to believe God, we laugh. Laughter may also indicate unbelief. We laugh because we simply do not believe what God said.

Challenge question:
Why are you laughing?

You cannot operate in radical faith to receive the promise of God until you deal with your laughter. God wants to know, "Why are you laughing?" Take the time to answer this question so that you are positioned to receive the promise of God.

God went back to the head. He didn't go to Sarah. He went to Abraham and He said, "Why is Sarah laughing?" God knew Sarah's laughter lay square on the shoulders of Abraham. Earlier Abraham laughed at God's promise "'*As for Sarai your wife, you are no longer to call her Sarai; her name will be Sarah. I will bless her and will surely give you a son by her. I will bless her so that she will be the mother of nations; kings of peoples will come from her. Abraham fell facedown; he laughed and said to himself, 'Will a son be born to a man a hundred years old? Will Sarah bear a child at the age of ninety? (Genesis 17:15-17)*'" Sarah learned from Abraham how to laugh at the promises of God. Men, we must pay close attention to how we respond to God's promises. Our wives are watching. Parents we must know that your children are watching our response to God's promises. When you laugh at the promises of God, you need know that everyone God has entrusted you with is going to laugh too. Husbands, if you laugh, your wife will laugh. Parents, if you laugh, your child will laugh.

God's next question was, "Is anything impossible for God?" I submit that this was a rhetorical question which God did not expect Abraham to answer. God already knew the answer. He just wanted Abraham and Sarah to remember. God's answer to Sarah's laughter was to remind her there is nothing too hard for God. God wants you to know there's nothing too hard for Him also.

Radical faith knows there's nothing too hard for God!

God didn't only ask the question; He gave a response: "I will return to you at the appointed time next year and Sarah will have a son." This was a declarative statement. It wasn't a statement of doubt. It was a statement made in assurance. "It's going to happen because I said it." God said, "My Word cannot go out and return back to me void." Every word that God speaks is obligated to come true. Therefore, if God told you that you will be free from depression and disease, you will be free. If He told you that you will have a mate, you will have a mate. If God told you He's going to make you financially stable, then you'll be financially stable. Whatever God said, it's done; it's already been settled in heaven. Our responsibility is to get in line with it in the earth realm.

Things may seem bleak right now. Instead of getting better, things may be getting worse. Perhaps every time you ask God to do something the opposite of what you ask for seems to happen. Maybe nothing is going your way. But God has declared it so. If God said it, that settles it. It's done! It's already accomplished. Now stand in radical faith!

Spiritual Principle: Radical faith trusts that what God said will come to pass

Don't Let Laughter Lead to You Lying

Sarah laughed, but God answered her laughter. He asked her the question and then He responded to her. Sarah was afraid, so she lied and said, "I did not laugh (Genesis 18:15."

It is very tempting to deny our laughter when we don't believe God at His word. But God says, "Don't deny it, own it." The only way you will come to believe is to deal with your doubt. We've already dealt with that. If you try to act like you don't doubt, you're not ready yet to receive the promise. If you're doubting, in denial, and being dishonest, you can't be delivered. But when you finally own your doubt, you're in prime position to receive what God has promised you. Sarah's laughter caused her to lie. She denied her laughter because of fear. Don't let your laughter cause you to lie because of fear. Admit it so that you can be delivered from doubt and receive what God has promised you.

News flash, God knows you laughed!

God said to Sarah, *"Yes, you did laugh. I heard you laugh. Even though you didn't laugh out loud, I heard it in your spirit. I know the thoughts you think before you ever think them. I know the dreams you have before you dream them. I know the plans you've made before they leave your mind. I'm God. I'm everywhere at the same time. I have all power and I know everything. I'm omniscient, I'm omnipotent, and I'm omnipresent. I heard you laugh"*

Challenge question:
What do you do when God confronts your denial?

Stop laughing and look to God! The Bible says, "I will look to the hills from which comes my help. All of my help comes from the Lord (Psalm 121:1 and 2)." You must stop laughing and start looking. Stop looking at your problems, stop looking at the circumstances, stop looking at the situation, and start looking at God. Many fail to receive the promise, because instead of looking up to God, they look inward at their own abilities or outward at the problem. They look at all the issues instead of looking at the One who is the Creator and the Redeemer.

Stop laughing and start looking at God. Then start listening to God. There are many voices that speak to us all the time. There are all kinds of voices that would have us to believe all kinds of things. Be careful whose voice you listen to. You must make sure that the voice you're listening to is the voice of God. If it does not line up with the Word of God, it's not God's voice. God's voice always acts in agreement with His Word.

Finally, start living as if the promise has already been received. Let this be your mindset "I can't see it yet. I don't know when it's going to manifest. A year seems like a long time. But I'm going to live like I already have it." One of my favorite stories is the little engine that could. You may remember the story. It's a children's book. Tommy was just a little engine. But he was an engine. One day, his dad, the big engine, got sick and couldn't pull the coal train up over the hill. So, the people came to Tommy and said, "Your daddy's sick and he can't pull the train today." Tommy said, "Oh, I can't do it. I can't do it. I'm just a little engine. I'm not big enough. I'm not strong enough. I don't have enough experience." But the people said, "Tommy, you can do it. You're an engine. Engines were created to pull trains up over hills." Tommy said, "You don't understand. I'm just a little engine. I'm too small. I'm not big enough. I'm not strong enough. I don't have enough experience." But the people kept saying, "Tommy, here's what you have to do. You have to believe that you can." Tommy said, "No, you don't understand. I'm just too small." That may be the lie the devil keeps whispering in your ear, every time God tells you His promises. He tells you it will never happen; you can't do it.

Stop listening to him and start looking to, listening to and living for God.

Tommy kept hearing, "You can do it, Tommy. You can do it, Tommy." Finally, somebody said, "Tommy, here's what I want you to do. As you get hooked up to the train, I want you to begin telling yourself, 'I think I can. I think I can.' As you make your first run up the hill, I want you to say, 'I think I can. I think I can.'" Tommy said, "What's that going to do?" His dad said, "Tommy, just try it." So, they backed Tommy up and they hooked him up. Tommy began saying, "I think I can. I think I can." He started moving a little bit. At every point Tommy said 'I think I can, I think I can. As Tommy said, "I think I can, I think I can" before he realized he pulled the train all the way up the hill and he as came down the other side and he was saying, "I knew I could. I knew I could." That's what we must do. We must become like Tommy. We have to say, "I know He will. I know He will. I know He will until the promise manifests. Then when the promise comes to pass, you have to say, "I knew He would. I knew He would."

Radical faith believes until the promise comes to pass!

From Barren to Blessed

"Now the LORD was gracious to Sarah as he had said, and the LORD did for Sarah what he had promised. Sarah became pregnant and bore a son to Abraham in his old age, at the very time God had promised him. Abraham gave the name Isaac to the son Sarah bore him. When his son Isaac was eight days old, Abraham circumcised him, as God commanded him. Abraham was a hundred years old when his son Isaac was born to him. Sarah said, 'God has brought me laughter, and everyone who hears about this will laugh with me.' And she added, 'Who would have said to Abraham that Sarah would nurse children? Yet I have borne him a son in his old age (Genesis 21:1-7).'"

She was in her late thirties when she started attending LTM. Her story was one of desire without fulfillment. She wanted two things—to be married and to have a baby. Neither seemed to be a possibility. As the years passed, her pain increased as she grew older and older. Finally, in 2017 she reached a place of resolved contentment that God may not allow her to get married or have a child. She was not giving up, but she was turning it over to God. Her prayer changed to Lord if it's your will that I get married, let my husband find me in your house serving you. We began praying together that the Lord would grant her request. Less than two weeks later her now husband walked into the building for assistance with a situation. The next Thursday he came to Bible study and heard her praying. His words were "I knew instantly that was my wife." A year later they were married. God turned her emptiness into fullness in an instant!

Understanding Barrenness

Barrenness is a state of emptiness. Barrenness is a state of wanting. It is a state of lack. For a woman in the ancient Near Eastern world during Sarah's day, it was, in essence, a sentence of ridicule, restlessness, and wretchedness. For a woman in ancient Israel, to be barren was to be cursed by God, it was for God to look at you and say, in their way of thinking, "You are incomplete. You are not whole. You are broken because you are barren." Children were seen as gifts from God, not much unlike our culture today. A child was a blessing, and a male child, particularly, was seen as the progenitor, or the antecedent of the progenitor. Therefore, a male child was a double blessing. *But barrenness was brokenness.* Perhaps as it relates to your relationship with God, your life dreams, your aspirations, or even to the things that you hoped to accomplish in your life, you feel barren and empty. You have been waiting on the manifestation of the promises of God. You've believed God for certain things to come forth in your life and they haven't manifested, and you feel empty. You may have even said to yourself, "My womb is empty. My dreams have not manifested. I am barren." You may have even asked, "God, what do I do with the emptiness?"

Barrenness produces an indescribable emptiness.

The Cry for Relief

When you are barren the only thing you really want is relief. The only thing that can relieve the emptiness of barrenness is a baby. Every person I have ever had the privilege of talking to who was barren had one driving question: when will I move from barren to blessed? Perhaps that is your cry today as you wait for the promises of God to come to pass in your life. It may be your cry as you watch others receive their promised blessing and you continue waiting for yours to manifest.

If that's the case, I have good news. I have discovered God does not mind answering our questions. We can go to God with whatever it is that is troubling us. If you listen intently and stay in the process, He will provide an answer. It may come in the sound of the mighty rushing wind. That's what He did on the day of Pentecost. It may come in the sound of a still, quiet voice. But if you keep listening long enough, God always gives an answer. I've learned it doesn't matter how dark the situation might seem, how dim it may appear, how dismal the outcome may be; God has an answer to your barrenness. He hears your cry and is prepared to take you from barren to blessed.

Stand in radical faith and watch God take you from barren to blessed!

It's Been a Long Time, but Not too Long

Abraham is now one hundred years old and Sarah is ninety. They've been on this journey towards a radical faith now for twenty-five years. They've been waiting for the promise since they left Haran twenty-five years ago. They've prayed. They've worshiped God. They've been through a great deal while waiting for God to keep His promise. Twenty-five years is a long time to wait. Yet through all of this, Abraham and Sarah did one thing that is critical to receiving the blessing God has promised you. It's what radical faith is all about.

What did they do?

Despite what may have seemed like complete procrastination on the part of God, Abraham and Sarah stayed in the process. They kept waiting. They stayed on the journey. They didn't quit.

Radical faith does not quit, it stays in the process

It's important that we understand something spiritually. It really doesn't matter how long God is taking, how long you've been going through what you're going through, or if it seems as though the promise is never going to come to pass. **You must not, you cannot, you dare not, quit the process.** When you quit the process, you cut off the promise. That bears repeating. When you quit the process and give up on God, you cut off the promise. The promise is dependent on you staying in the process. You must stay on the journey. If you have fallen down, get back up and keep going. If the enemy has attacked you and gotten you off course, get back on course. It doesn't matter how many times you fall down; you win if you don't quit.

Remember: You Win If You Don't Quit

You lose only when you quit the process. Perhaps you feel as if you are taking one step forward and two steps backward. It doesn't matter. Make up your mind, to stay in the process until you go from barren to blessed. Make up your mind that you will not quit. Job's wife told him, "You ought to just curse God and die." But Job said, "Woman, you sound foolish. You don't sound like my wife. The Lord gives and the Lord takes away. Naked I came into the world, and naked I shall depart. But blessed be the name of the Lord (Job 2:9 and 10)." In essence Job said, "there's no way I'm going to quit." You have to reach the point where you say, "I don't care how long I have to hang on, I'm going to hang on. I'll tie another knot onto the end of the rope and keep hanging on. Because as long as I stay in the process, I know I'm going to get blessed. I will stay in the process." Make that your declaration today!

Challenge questions:
Are you determined to stay in the process no matter how long it takes?
Will you wait for God to take you from barren to blessed?

The Process

We must understand the process. God came at the appointed time: "Now the LORD was gracious to Sarah as he had said, and the LORD did for Sarah what he had promised. Sarah became pregnant and bore a son to Abraham in his old age, *at the very time God had promised him* (Genesis 21:1 and 2)." This lets us know there's a set time. Your blessing has an appointed time. Every promise of God has a set time of manifestation. A set time is also known as a season. We must learn how to wait for the set time. You can try to take matters into your own hands, to bring the season to pass, but it will not happen until God says, "It's now the time." Abraham can testify to this. He and Sarah took matters into their own hands and tried to rush the manifestation of the promise. The end result was Ishmael. What happens when you try to rush the appointed time? You go from being blessed to burdened. You cannot rush God's timing. One of the things we must learn is God has a season for everything. Ecclesiastics 3:1-8 says "There is a time for everything, and a season for every activity under heaven: a time to be born and a time to die, a time to plant and a time to uproot…a time to love and a time to hate, a time for war and a time for peace." There's a season for every activity. Right now, you may be in your dry season. It's important to know, just because you're in your dry season doesn't mean God's not with you, it doesn't mean your blessing is not coming. You've got to know it's just a season.

It's just a season!

You're in a season right now, but know that at the appointed time, God is coming. Everyone's appointed time is different. But if we stay in the process and wait on His appointed time, God will bring the promise to pass. Listen to the words "…and the Lord visited Sarah at the appointed time." How do we know it was the appointed time? Genesis 18:9 and 10 records, "Where is your wife Sarah?' they asked him. 'There, in the tent,' he said. Then the LORD said, 'I will surely return to you about this time next year, and Sarah your wife will have a son.'" These words are important. They reveal God has a specific time in mind for bringing His promise to pass. No matter how long you've been waiting rest in knowing God will bring the promise to pass at His appointed time, "Now the LORD was gracious to Sarah as he had said, and the LORD did for Sarah what he had promised. Sarah became pregnant and bore a son to Abraham in his old age, at the very time God had promised him (Genesis 21:1 and 2)." This is so powerful! What God said He was going to do, is exactly what He did! How does that help us? What God promised He would bless you with, is exactly what He will give you.

The Only Disqualifying Act

There is one disqualifying act that will keep you from receiving the promise. It may not be what you think at all. The only disqualifying act is quitting. Do not mistake this for a license to live in disobedience to the will of God. While you are not disqualified by your disobedience, there are definite consequences for it. Yet, if you stay in the process, even though you might fall sometimes, you might have faith failures, you might make some bad choices, the end result is at the appointed time, God will show up to bless you. You will go from being barren to blessed. Don't let the enemy deceive you into believing you are disqualified from receiving the promise because you fell down. God hasn't changed His mind!

The Baby is Here, Now What?

Can't you hear Abraham and Sarah, "So now we have a baby, what shall we name him? I don't know. But I remember that you laughed on the day at the tent, when God said He was going to give us a son. Well, it seems to me now that God is laughing. We know that He who laughs last laughs loudest. Why don't we name him Isaac, which, when translated, means "He is laughing" because while we may have laughed when God promised us the blessing, He is now laughing with us." God doesn't laugh at us He laughs with us. Isaac was God's laughter in the life of Abraham and Sarah.

God rejoices when He blesses you.

Challenge questions:
Do you realize that God is happy to bless you?
How does it feel knowing God rejoices with you when He blesses you?

Somehow, we accept the lie that God doesn't want us blessed. We are deceived into believing that God wants us to be messed up and miserable; that God wants us to be broke, busted, and disgusted; He wants us to be depressed, down and in the depths of despair. But the truth is God wants to take you from barren to blessed and to laugh with you. God is waiting to give you the blessing so stay in the process. Because, in due season, God is going to laugh with you. He is ready to explode in joyous laughter with you as He brings forth the promised blessing in your life! Rejoice in knowing God wants to laugh with you.

Radical faith knows God is delighted to laugh with us

Our Responsibility is to be Obedient with the Blessing

He laughs. That's the name. "He laughs." What a name. "He laughs." Please know that when the blessing comes, you still have an obligation. There are times when God has blessed us, and we have not been obedient with the blessing. We have abused the blessing. We have neglected the blessing. We have misused the blessing. We have failed to obey God in how we treat our blessing. When Abraham received his son, at eight days old, he circumcised Him as the Lord had commanded. Just because you've gone from barren to blessed doesn't mean you can stop being obedient. There are those who have been blessed by God that have not been obedient with the blessing. Perhaps you are asking, "What do you mean?"

Three areas we tend to disobey when blessed by God:

Our wealth
Our relationships
Our worship

It is easy when God blesses us with financial increase to disobey Him in our giving into the Kingdom. We rationalize why we cannot afford to give generously. We begin spending our wealth on things in the world instead of the things of God. Don't cut off your blessing by being disobedient with your wealth.

It is also easy to disobey God when He blesses our relationships. The biggest way I see this happen is when a person begins putting the relationship above God. It can happen subtly. The person begins devoting more and more time to the relationship until God has been placed on the back burner.

We must be careful also not to disobey God in the area of worship. Worship is our act of service to the Lord. It is how we respond to and honor God for who He is. Worship is how we live on a daily basis, not simply what we do on Sunday morning. It is easy to be deceived into believing that we can worship God in our own way and on our own terms. We think because we have the Holy Spirit operating in our lives, we can pick and choose when and how to worship God.

The danger of disobeying God when you have received the blessing is that it leads you to abuse, misuse, and/or neglect the blessing. In doing so you may end up forfeiting the blessing. Don't forfeit the blessing you waited so long to receive by disobeying God in how you treat it. Remember, you can't do God's will your way. There's only one way to do God's will, and that's God's way.

Challenge questions:
How have you been guilty of disobeying God with your blessings?
What needs to change so that you obey God with the blessings you've received?

The Cause of Laughter

I want to share one final insight regarding the birth of Isaac. "Abraham was a hundred years old when his son Isaac was born to him. Sarah said, 'God has brought me laughter, and everyone who hears about this will laugh with me (Genesis 21:5 and 6).'" The question could be raised, "Why was Sarah laughing and why are they laughing with her?" Let me see if I can make sense of this by sharing a personal example.

I do my own hair and I do a pretty good job. But occasionally, I go to the barbershop. When you are at the barbershop there is a person sitting in the chair. The barber does his hair and when he is done, the patron looks in the mirror, likes what he sees and pays the barber. The barber then says next. The next customer sits down, and the barber goes through the same process. He cuts the person's hair and when finished says, next. This happens repeatedly. Every person in the barbershop understands that their turn is coming. Each time the barber says next, each customer knows my turn is getting closer.

I submit that the reason they laughed with Sarah was because they reasoned that if God would keep His promise to Sarah and bless her, then they could be sure that their turn was coming to be blessed. Learn to rejoice with others who are receiving the promise God has made them knowing that your turn is coming. Say to yourself "I'm next!" We can rejoice with others knowing the same God who blessed them will also bless us. Romans 12:15 declares, "Rejoice with those who rejoice. Mourn with those who mourn." When others receive what God has promised them, laugh and rejoice with them, knowing your blessing is on the way!

Radical faith rejoices with others!

Sarah said, "They laughed with me. They didn't laugh at me." Before everybody laughed at Sarah. "She's barren. Look at her. She's not whole. Look at her, that's a sinful woman. Look at her, she's empty. Look at her, she's sick on the inside. Her womb is dried up." Perhaps everyone in your life has been laughing at you saying, he/she will never receive what God has promised. But I promise you, if you stay in the process, in due season they won't be laughing at you anymore, they'll start laughing with you because they will know you are blessed and highly favored of the Lord.

You Will Nurse the Promised Blessing

We find these words in Genesis 21:7 "She also said, "'Who would have said to Abraham that Sarah would nurse children. For I have borne him a son in his old age.'" When a woman has a healthy pregnancy and her body is functioning properly, at birth or shortly thereafter, her breasts fill up with milk. She then has the nutrients necessary to nourish the baby. Sarah was ninety years old. Her womb was barren. Humanly, it was an impossibility for her to give birth. Perhaps you're sitting in the state of impossibility. It appears there's no way the blessing is going to come forth out of a barren womb. Know this, not only did God open Sarah's womb to bring forth a baby, He caused her mammary glands to produce milk in ninety-year-old breasts in order that Sarah might be able to provide the necessary nutrients through her body to nourish her blessing. When God blesses you, He will put in you everything necessary to bring the blessing to maturity. Some would say, "So what, that's that just natural." No, it's supernatural because God can take our mess and all of our mess-ups in order take us from being barren to blessed. He can also produce in us, in a spiritual way, everything we need to nurture, develop and mature the blessing. That's a gift. It's something only God can do. Only God can give you what you need to nurture and nourish your blessing.

You might think that just because God has produced the blessing, you can now do whatever you want to do, go wherever you want to go, and live however you want to live. The truth is unless you stay connected to God, what you need to nourish, nurture and mature your blessing will never come to pass. You must rely on the Promise Keeper to do in you what is necessary to bring your blessing to maturity. The One who blessed you is the only One who can keep you. The One who birthed the blessing is the One who can bring the blessing to maturity. The One who gave you the promise is the One who will fulfill the promise. So, what do we do? *We stay in the process. We trust God to show up at the appointed time. We obey once we receive the blessing.*

We rely on God to do through us, to give us, to produce in us, everything necessary to nurture, nourish, and mature the blessing. In doing so, we receive from God all that He's promised.

Trust God to fill you with what's necessary to bring the blessing to maturity!

The Final Test

"Now it came about after these things, that God tested Abraham, and said to him, "Abraham!" And he said, "Here I am." He said, "Take now your son, your only son, whom you love, Isaac, and go to the land of Moriah, and offer him there as a burnt offering on one of the mountains of which I will tell you." So Abraham rose early in the morning and saddled his donkey, and took two of his young men with him and Isaac his son; and he split wood for the burnt offering, and arose and went to the place of which God had told him (Genesis 22:1-3 NASB)."

Our daughter Lydia started walking very early. By nine months old she was walking so well we had to do another level of childproofing for our home. One of the childproofing strategies was to place a portable dishwasher in front of the basement doorway so that she could not get to the stairs because there was no door. One evening after returning home, I was distracted by my cell phone and before I could put the dishwasher in front of the door Lydia slipped past me and preceded to walk down the stairs. It didn't go well. When she hit the second step she began falling. My wife screamed and ran to our bedroom hysterical. I ran down the stairs praying she was okay. Lydia let out a loud, ear-piercing yell and then began crying uncontrollably. I feared the worse—that our gift from God was seriously injured. To our delight she only suffered a small scrape on her elbow and a slight cut on her lip. God proved His faithfulness to us that day. I learned two valuable lessons—don't be distracted and God is always faithful to His promises.

It Seems Unfair, but It's True

Imagine with me if you will, waiting twenty-five for God to fulfill the promise He made you. The promise has now come to pass, and you are enjoying the pleasure of living with it. As you finally begin to relax and enjoy the reality of life with the promise, God appears again. This time instead of God making a promise, He has a request. The request is simple, "I want you to go sacrifice the promise."

Challenge questions:
How would you respond?
What would you say?
What would you do?
What thoughts would be running through your head?

I imagine I would immediately conclude God was being unfair and unreasonable. It would make no sense. Why would God give me the promise, only to take it away? I would likely be angry and extremely upset with God. What about you?

That is exactly what God did to Abraham. Approximately twelve years after Isaac was born, God showed up and asked Abraham to take him and offer him as a sacrifice. This request must have seemed unfair to Abraham, but it was true. God really did ask him to sacrifice Isaac. This request forms the backdrop for our final examination of what it means to have radical faith. As we examine this act of faith, may we find courage and strength to trust God with our blessing.

God Tests Us

There's always a test!

Here's a reality: God tests us! I know that doesn't sound spiritual or very theological, but it's true. I am convinced that God tests us to measure the degree to which the information given has been received and retained. By now, Abraham had walked with God over thirty years. He's endured faith failures, let Lot go, and learned how to live with Ishmael. Now God wanted to show Abraham how much he had progressed in his faith. Perhaps you may be going through your own test of faith. God may have you in a place where you are discovering just how much you have progressed in your faith. If so, I pray these words will help you navigate successfully through the test. If you are not in a place of testing, my prayer is that you will hold on to these words so that when the test comes you will pass with flying colors.

There's scriptural support for the assertion that God tests us. In James 1:2-4 we read these words:
"My brethren, count it all joy when you fall into various trials, knowing that the testing of your faith produces patience. But let patience its perfect work, that you may be perfect (mature) and complete, lacking nothing."

The reality is when we say yes to God, there will come a point when our faith will be tested. It is not a matter of if your faith will be tested, it is a matter of when. Not only does the test measure the degree to which you have received and retained the information given, it also teaches you how to live in radical faith.

Until one's faith has been tested, it cannot be trusted.

Let me share a personal example. In November of 2004, after five years on my job, the company I was working for began merging with another company. The position I was in an Assistant Director of the agency was being eliminated and I would have to reapply for a new position with the new organization. I begin seeking God regarding what to do. I sensed that God would not have me continue on with the new agency, but I knew our small ministry could not support my family and me on a full-time basis. I prayed earnestly and heard from the Lord my season was up. It made no sense seeing that I did not have any clear strategies for replacing my nearly six-figure income as the primary wage earner in our home. On February 1, 2005 when the merger was official, I worked my last day for a secular company. God was clear, you will have to trust me in this. Let me tell you, fourteen years later I have still not worked for another company. God has sustained our family. It has been very hard at times. I've even considered finding a job. Yet each time God has said trust me in this. My faith has been tested and as a result my faith is more radical today than it has ever been. I know God always keeps His promises!

The Test

What was Abraham's test? God told him to sacrifice the blessing he had been promised. God was very clear and did not indicate any plan to preserve Isaac. What God told Abraham to do made no sense from a human perspective.

"Take your son, your only son, and offer him there as a burnt offering on one of the mountains of which I will tell you (Genesis 22:1 and 2)." The request surely had to test Abraham's logic as well as his trust in God. Why would God ask him to sacrifice the blessing he waited twenty-five years to receive? Not only that, but why would God command Abraham to do something that was outside of God's character? God had never required or condoned human sacrifice. Yet, He asked Abraham to offer his son to Him. What was God doing?

When we are tested it is important to figure out what God is doing. The only way to do that, is to do what the Lord asks you to do. Often, we fail to learn what God is doing because when He calls us to do something that doesn't make sense, we allow our human reasoning to override our faith and do not do what God has asked.

You will never know what God is doing, until you do what He asks you to do!

Not only did the test not make sense from a human standpoint; not only was it outside of God's character; it was also painful and personal. Listen again to the words the Lord spoke, "Take your son, your only son." There are two implications in this statement: God only saw Isaac as the son of promise (only son) and God intended for Abraham to sacrifice Isaac. Here is a reality; God has the right to ask us to give up anything He wants us to. Let that sink in. We often want to put God in a box around how He can and can't behave. Yet as the creator of all who is sovereign, God can act however He wants to act. If God chooses to allow your son you waited twenty-five to receive to be sacrificed on an altar, He is within His sovereign right to do so. This is hard, especially for western saints who want a God we can control.

> **The test is trusting God enough to do what He says even when it doesn't make sense!**

Challenge question:
What would you do if God asked you to give up something or someone you waited decades to receive?

The Response

How did Abraham respond? *"So Abraham rose early in the morning and saddled his donkey and took two of his young men with him and Isaac his son; and he split the wood for the burnt offering, and arose and went to the place of which God had told him (Genesis 22:3)."* At this point I would have expected Abraham to raise some questions to God. It seems to me that Abraham would have been justified in giving God some push back. After all, what kind of God asks a person to sacrifice their son after waiting all that time to receive him? Yet, Abraham doesn't ask any questions. He simply got up the next morning, prepared all he would need, saddled up his donkey, gathered his servants and his son, and set out for the place that God told him to go. Wow! That's living in radical faith.

> **Radical faith does what God asks even when you don't understand**

Many times, we do not experience the awesomeness of God because we can't move forward in faith unless we understand exactly why God is asking us to do something.

We get frozen by our own thinking and miss out on God's miraculous moves.

I remember this almost happening to us. In 2010 our ministry was gifted two buildings by a local bank. As a ministry without significant resources the gift was a blessing and a burden. First, we had to raise the money to renovate the property to secure occupancy. After finally doing that, just as we were planning our grand opening of the LTM Freedom Center, we received notice from the City that the building had an outstanding water bill to the tune of nearly $6,000 that was left by the previous owner. We had less than 30 days to raise the money. Honestly, I was ready to give up! Yet God said trust me in this. We started a capital campaign not sure if we could raise the money in 30 days. We prayed and trusted that God would not allow us to lose the blessing after He gave it to us. We were still short of the needed funds a day before the cut off day. That day the money we needed came in so that we could go to City Hall and pay the debt on the final day! God again proved He could be trusted.

Radical faith allows us to act on the word of God without requiring an explanation. That's what Abraham did! "God said it, I will do it, even if it doesn't make sense." That is the type of faith God wants us to have. The type that obeys even when it doesn't make sense from a logical standpoint. I must be careful here that I do not send the message that I am talking about uninformed or blind faith. Abraham did not have either. He knew through experience that trusting God would always prove the right option. Abraham had spent over thirty years trusting God!

My former pastor, Bishop Joseph W. Walker, III would tell us that we need a faith file. A mental file of all the times God has come through in the past. I've discovered through the years that this is absolutely true. We can act in radical faith because we know God has always come through!

Genesis 22:5 states *"Abraham said to the young men, 'Stay here with the donkey, and I and the lad will go over there; and we will worship and return to you.'"* That was a statement of radical faith. Abraham didn't know how, but he was confident God was going to work out the situation so that he and Isaac returned safely after they worshiped. In Hebrews 11:17-19 we read these words as it relates to Abraham's faith in this moment *"By faith Abraham, when he was tested, offered up Isaac, and he who had received the promises was offering up his only begotten Son, it was he to whom it was said, "IN ISAAC YOUR DESCENDANTS SHALL BE CALLED." He considered that God is able to raise people even from the dead, from which he also received him back as a type."* Abraham trusted God to the point that he believed God was able to raise Isaac from the dead if He had to in order to keep His promise. That is the place of faith to which God wants us to get. He wants our trust in Him to be so strong that we are willing to do whatever He calls us to do. That is radical faith. Radical faith causes us to trust God for the impossible. It causes us to believe that God can do the undoable.

Radical faith is trusting God enough to do whatever He calls us to do!

The Question

As Abraham and Isaac made their way to the place that God told Abraham to build the altar and make the sacrifice, it suddenly dawned on Isaac that something was missing.

Listen to his question to his father, "My Father... Behold the fire and the wood, but where is the lamb for the burnt offering?" Isaac realized that one cannot worship without a sacrifice! That is a truth that many need to understand. In Romans 12:1 we read, "Therefore I urge you, brethren, by the mercies of God, to present your bodies a living and holy sacrifice, acceptable to God, which is your spiritual service of worship." There can be no worship without a sacrifice. Isaac said, "Daddy where is the sacrifice?"

Abraham's response again revealed his level of faith. He said to Isaac, "God will provide for Himself the lamb for the burnt offering, my son." Talk about trust! Abraham's faith was so radical that he fully expected God to work out the provision of the sacrifice. When we have radical faith, we trust God to do whatever needs to be done in order for us to carry out the assignment He has given us. Therefore, we must understand that the test is for your development not your destruction. God gets no glory in destroying you. God's purpose in the test is to prove your faith. He wants you to believe Him for things that seem impossible.

Radical faith believes God for that which seems impossible!

You don't have the power to retain the blessing. If you didn't have the power to produce it, then you don't have the power to keep it. Abraham realized the only hope he had for keeping his blessing was to do what God said even if it didn't make sense. He said, "...God himself will provide the sacrifice." That was a statement of radical faith. It was a statement of a person completely dependent on God. That is where God wants to get us.

Challenge questions:
Will you trust God enough to do what He says even when it doesn't make sense?
Are you confident in God's ability to preserve the blessing?

The Act of Worship

When Abraham and Isaac arrived at the designated place to offer the sacrifice, four things happened:

Abraham built an altar
He placed the wood in order
He bound Isaac and placed him on the altar
He stretched out his hand to slay Isaac

Was Abraham really going to go through with it? Was he really going to kill his son?

Everything in the passage says Abraham was going to slay Isaac as an act of worship unto God. We learn a great deal from this act of worship.

- Worship is not offering God what we want to offer Him, it is offering Him what he requires.
- Worship grows out of trust.
- There can be no worship without sacrifice.
- Worship requires obedience to the point of personal pain.
- There is no sacrifice too great for God.

Worship is the act of surrender and service to God. Abraham had learned to worship God. He was willing to give up his son as an act of worship. He had a no-limits mindset when it came to worshiping God. Radical faith produces in us a no-limits mindset when it comes to worshiping God. We humbly proclaim, "All to Jesus I surrender, all to Him I freely give."

Radical faith produces a no-limits mindset when it comes to worshiping God!

The Lord Will Provide

As Abraham lifted his hand to slay Isaac, something amazing happen. Try to visualize this father with his son bound and lying on an altar. The wood stacked together to quickly catch fire. The knife in his hand lifted toward the sky.

Challenge questions:
What would have been going through your mind?
What emotions would you be feeling?
What do you think Isaac would be thinking?

It was in that moment that God stepped in to stop Abraham. "Then the angel of the Lord called to him from heaven and said, "Abraham, Abraham!" and he said, "Here I am (Genesis 22:11)." What an amazing divine interruption! God spoke just as Abraham was about to swing the knife to kill the blessing. What did God say to Abraham in that moment? These are words that prove Abraham had arrived at the place to which God was leading him. They are words which every servant of the Lord should long to hear. "... do not stretch out your hand against the lad, and do nothing to him; for now, I know that you fear God, since you have not withheld your son, your only son from me (Genesis 22:12)." Did it really take that for God to know Abraham feared Him? Was this really all about God wanting to see how far He could push Abraham to prove his trust? I am convinced that isn't what the test was all about. Abraham proved his faith was radical. He was willing to kill his only son at the voice of the Lord. Surely the all-knowing God had to know that already? Of course, He did.

I am convinced the test wasn't for God's sake; but it was for Abraham's. I'm convinced the purpose of the test was to show Abraham how radical his faith had become. This was not the same man who twenty-five years earlier told Sarah to tell the king she was his sister. This was not the same man who went in to sleep with Hagar because he didn't completely trust God would bring forth a son through the loins of Sarah. Nor was this the same man who laughed when God told him that he and Sarah would have a son. This was a man with radical faith.

The message for us in this passage is that the test is for our sake not God's. The purpose of the test is to show us how radical our faith has become. When we are tested, God wants us to see how much we trust Him. Never think for a moment that God doesn't know how much you trust Him. Of course, He does! He wants you to know it also.

I remember early on in our marriage. I was really struggling to trust my wife. I had been through a very painful marriage and divorce. I was in a place where I wasn't sure I ever wanted to trust a woman that much again. One morning while praying in the shower, I shared with the Lord that I was really struggling to trust my wife. I will never forget what I heard in my spirit from the Lord. He said, "I'm not asking you to trust her, I'm asking you to trust me." As the tears flowed, I was blown away. I told the Lord I would make myself vulnerable to my wife and trust her because I trusted His ability to keep me safe. It changed my marriage! Over twenty years later I am still trusting God in my marriage and I learn to be more vulnerable every day with my wife.

As Abraham heard the words the angel of the Lord spoke, he lifted his eyes and saw a ram in the thicket behind him. Abraham believed God once again. He looked for the provision God made so that he didn't have to kill his son. When we have radical faith, we look for the provision that God has made to keep us from destroying what He promised us.

The good news is the Lord always provides! Genesis 22:14 states "Abraham called the name of that place The Lord Will Provide, as it is said to this day, 'In the mount of the Lord it will be provided.'" Anyone who has been a believer any length of time is familiar with the Hebrew form of this *Jehovah Jireh*. God always provides for those who operate in radical faith. I have seen Him do it over and over again in my life and in the lives of others. We must realize that radical faith positions us to experience God's miraculous provision. Experiencing God's miraculous provision causes us to praise Him.

Radical faith knows the test will end in praise to God for His provision!

The Blessing of Passing the Test

There is one other thought we need to consider before concluding our journey with Abraham to radical faith. Genesis 22:15-22 records God renewing His covenant with Abraham. The timing of the renewal of the covenant is significant. God said "... By Myself I have sworn, declares the Lord, because you have done this thing and have not withheld your son, your only son... (22:16)" What God was about to say to Abraham was based on his response to the test. That lets us know that when we pass the test, God's promises to us are renewed because of radical faith. God said "...indeed I will greatly bless you, and I will greatly multiply your seed as the stars of the heavens and as the sand which is on the seashore; and your seed shall possess the gate of their enemies. In your seed all the nations of the earth shall be blessed, because you have obeyed my voice (Genesis 22:17 and 18)."

There are four aspects of God's promise to Abraham renewed in this passage:

- Extraordinary blessing
- Abundant seed
- Victory over his enemies
- All nations would be blessed through Him

What is the significance of these promised blessings?

They were the same blessings that God promised Abraham over nearly forty years ago when He left Haran. God never changed His mind about the promise. Even though it had taken almost forty years, the promise was still intact. The blessing of passing the test is that everything God has promised us is renewed! This lets us know that no matter how long it takes, when we operate in radical faith to pass the test, the promises will come to pass.

Radical faith positions us to receive God's promises no matter how long it takes!

God said the reason He was renewing His promise to Abraham was because of his obedience. Wait a minute you say, God never told Abraham that the promise was contingent on his obedience. Actually, God did tell Abraham that very thing at the very beginning. God is calling Abraham to leave everything familiar and go to a place He would show him said that if he did it then all the promises would be his. *Radical faith is obedient faith.*

Abraham had radical faith. He was willing to sacrifice his son because God said so. If you want to experience the promises of God, you must have a faith radical enough to obey God to the point of sacrificing everything He has given you because He says so. That is radical faith!

One final word of encouragement as we move forward in radical faith. "So Abraham returned to the young men, and they arose and went together to Beersheba; and Abraham lived at Beersheba (Genesis 22:19)." What is the point of this verse and what does it have to do with radical faith? The very thing Abraham declared by faith would happen when they arrived at the place of the sacrifice was exactly what happened. Abraham said he and Isaac were going to worship God and return. Abraham and Isaac went and worshiped God and returned. Radical faith moves us to declare what we expect God to do and then see it manifest. Before you dismiss me as a name it and claim it, overly spiritualizing, religious fanatic, listen to the words of Hebrews 11:1 and 2 "Now faith is the assurance of things hoped for, the conviction of things not seen. For by it men of old gained approval."

Faith is the assurance of what has not manifested and confidence concerning what we haven't yet seen. Abraham spoke in faith and saw what he said come to pass.

As you go forth in radical faith, speak exactly what God calls you to speak and watch it come to pass. That is radical faith!

www.ingramcontent.com/pod-product-compliance
Lightning Source LLC
Chambersburg PA
CBHW071848070526
44583CB00016B/1592